MYSTIC EXPERIENCES

TALES OF
YOGA AND VEDANTA

MYSTIC EXPERIENCES

TALES OF
YOGA AND VEDANTA
FROM
THE YOGA VASISHTHA

BY

BHAGAVAN DAS

With Notes by Dr. ANNIE BESANT

GYAN

Published by

Gyan Publishing House
5, Ansari Road
Daryaganj, New Delhi-110002
Phone: 011-47034999, 9811692060
E-mail: books@gyanbooks.com

Distribution Network
gyanbooks.com
India, USA, Canada, UK, Australia

ISBN: 978-93-6208-176-6 (PB)
First Published, 1944

2nd Impression 2024

Printed at: Gyan Press, Delhi.

MYSTIC EXPERIENCES TALES OF YOGA AND VEDANTA
Author: BHAGAVAN DAS, NOTES BY ANNIE BESANT

MYSTIC EXPERIENCES

TALES OF

YOGA AND VEDANTA

FROM

THE YOGA VASISHTHA

BY

BHAGAVAN DAS

Author of 'The Science of Peace', 'The Science of Emotions', 'The Science of Social Organisation in India,'

With Notes by Dr. Annie Besant

THE INDIAN BOOKSHOP

THEOSOPHICAL SOCIETY, BENARES CITY

INDIA

1928

FOREWORD

Two histories the Sage Valmiki wrote to teach the growing world he loved so well the way of virtue and of happiness. The one, intended for the younger souls, depicts the outer life of Rama, prince and King of Avadha, in the North, and tells of how he warred against and slew the evil King, Ravana, of the South. This ancient book is known to all the world as the Ramayana. The other, helpful at a later stage, is called the Maha Ramayana, Greater Book, and it describes the inner life of Rama, telling how he triumphed over foes within himself, and so prepared to fight and conquer, for the helping of the world, the outer evil forces rampant in that time.

The story of this Greater Book is here essayed in brief.

PREFATORY NOTE

The Yoga-Vasishtha, a Samskrit work, in thirty-two thousand *shlokas*, or sixty-six thousand lines, is highly honored among Indian Vedantins, for its philosophy and its hints on practical mysticism, as also its literary beauty and poetry. The saying about it, among the Vedantins, is that it is a work of the *siddh-avastha*, *i. e.*, for the philosopher-yogi, who, having mastered the theory, is passing on to the practice of it; while the other well-known works, even the *Gita*, the *Upanishats*, and the *Brahm-sutras*, are works of the *sadhan-avastha*, *i.e.*, for those who are yet trying to master the theory.

The very highly abbreviated version, of about a sixth of the work, which is here presented to the public, originally appeared in *The Theosophical Review* (of London, then edited by Mrs. Annie Besant and Mr. G. R. S. Mead), in 1899-1901 Mrs. Besant very kindly added some valuable notes which greatly elucidate some very obscure portions of the Story of Lila.

Friends have, from time to time, wished that the tales were rescued from the oblivion of the pages of a periodical. The present General Secretary of the Indian Section of the Theosophical Society, Pandit Iqbal Narain Gurtu, kindly expressed the desire to fulfil that wish, through the Publishing Department of the Section. Thus the tales are re-appearing after having slept for nearly thirty years. I have revised them, but with scarcely any alterations. There has been no opportunity to submit her notes to Mrs. Besant, for revision. They have been printed exactly as they first appeared.

Benares
October 1, 1927

BHAGAVAN DAS

BOOK I

RAMA'S VAIRAGYA

CHAPTER I

The Dying of Desire

Rama, in the first exuberant and beauteous bloom of youth, with the whole world around wearing its most attractive hues for him, eldest son of Dasha ratha, over-lord of all earth's Kings, heir to the glories of the Solar Race of Rulers that abided on the earth only to teach to other kings the duties of their office—unto Rama, while engaged in going round the Tirthas, shrines and sacred places of the land, at the early age of sixteen years, came Vairagya, exhaustion of the outward-leading forces of Desire, and revulsion from attachment to all things that perish. He heard the call of the Eternal from whose presence he had wandered forth. He heard the call, and not yet understanding its full meaning, turned his face towards his home from his pleasure wanderings and sports in the fair places of the earth.

There, in his royal home, the prince's large-eyed face grew daily larger-eyed with wistfulness and pining for he knew not what yet clearly; and he sat in sadness in his palace with no heart for anything; or if he moved, then languid and laborious, at much urging of his loyal kinsfolk, even for the doing of the daily duties ordered for his race by his great forefather Manu.

Then they told the king, his father, how his loved son's face grew pale and paler every day. And the king was full of care, and called the prince and asked him tenderly: "What is the longing, O my son, that so distresses thee?" And he asked him this repeatedly, but Rama always answered: "Nothing."

CHAPTER II

The Coming of the Master

Then the king went to the Sage Vasishtha, to him who was the Teacher of the Solar Kings, and to whom and to whose race has been assigned the work of holding and expounding on this earth, during this Kalpa-eon, the Science of the Highest. And the Sage consoled the king saying that wrath and sadness and rejoicing came not for small cause unto the good.

The king went back unto his halls, taking the

Sage with him to see the prince, and sat thinking upon those words of his, unsatisfied and doubtful. But even as he sat so lost in care the warders of the palace-gates announced the Rishi Vishwamitra standing at those gates accompanied by other sages and disciples. Hastening out to do due honour to the Sage, the monarch saw that grand and glorious form, casting forth light on all sides like the sun, and crowned with matted yellow locks like flames of fire, tinging the palace-guard, with all its flags and cars and elephants and horses, with a bright glow of gold, combining in one shining frame the Tejas (1) of the Brahmana with the Ojas (2) of the Kshattriya, looking like some large mountain-peak of snow, with head enveloped in a sunset-lightened haze of clouds; tranquil and all-gentle, yet inspiring awe; calm-fronted, happy, peaceful, yet disturbing the beholder's mind with new and vague emotions of reverence and humility and wonder; sprinkling the people, in sweet words and gracious glances, with sprays of that compassion which over-filled his mind as limpid waters fill the mountain-lake.

The monarch saw and bent low till his forehead touched those holy feet, and meekly led them in,

(1) Splendour, lustre.

(2) Energy, vitality.

and, offering service, begged for task to do, and said he would perform.

And Vishwamitra asked that Rama should be given to him for a space to help in the performance of high sacrifices wherein Kshattriya help was indispensable to Brahmana.

Then the king told Vishwamitra how his son was listless with an unknown malady; and sent for him and placed him there before the Sage.

CHAPTER III

The Questioning and Prayer

Vishwamitra asked the prince, " What ails thee ?" And the prince replied in words, slow with their weight of meaning, but flowing in a stayless stream of stores long gathered :

" Bhagavan !, Great and Holy One !, since thou askest me I answer thee, for none, however mannerless, may dare gainsay the Great Ones. Here in my father's mansions was I born, and brought up here, and here I studied what was taught to me. Thereafter, following carefully the ways of truth and virtue, I travelled over all the ocean-girdled earth. And by the time I brought my travels to a close, reflection rose within me strongly and swept away my interest in the world, and ever since I take no pleasure in the things of life, and always I am pondering within myself—What is this that men call pleasure? What is pain? What is this expanse and series of Samsara, endless world-procession?

"The world is born to die, and dies to reappear, and everything but passes, nothing stays. And all the world is but the play of mind; and that, we see, is false. Who, then, has cast this glamour on our eyes and made blind playthings of us? Always are we running as the deer run for the mirage-water in the desert, and always do we find that water turning into sand at near approach. And as I think of this and who I am and whence, I find no pleasure in these large dominions, nor any in the enjoyments that they can supply.

"Do thou expound to me, O Sage!, what is it, this that dies, this that is born again and grows? What are old age and death and evil fortune, and birth and riches, disappearance and appearance? How may pain cease? Such are the thoughts that haunt me night and day, and the great misery of the world weighs like a stone upon my heart, and often should I weep aloud except for fear of my own kinsfolk. Such are my ailments; such the malady that embitters for me all sweet things of life. Thinking of the many pains that hedge round every pleasure, my mind can find no peace, and frets unceasingly, like the wild forest elephant newly put in chains.

"O Muni! (1), men invented wealth to ease their pains. But Lakshmi (2), fickle, thankless, gives not ease, but ever breeds heart-burning, discontent and greed and greater misery; ever leaving man when most he wants her, ever paying back his love with laugh of scorn.

"And Life itself, for which we beg and crave so cringingly and piteously and meanly, life is fickle as the droplets trembling on the edges of wind-shaken leaves. More sensible is it to try to bind the winds; more sensible is it to try to break up space; more sensible is it to try to wear the running river's ripples as a wreath; it is not sensible at all to place faith in our faithless lives! No love of life is left in me, O Muni!

"Men find enjoyment in the play of Pride. How may I speak out all its pettiness! The I, the I, ever

(1) Ascetic; Originally, an ascetic who had taken the vow of silence.

(2) Goddess of wealth and prosperity.

the empty I! When I consider how from utter emptiness it takes its birth, and grows and flourishes therein, and how from its vacuity there flows full store of miseries and evils for all men, I have no heart to speak of I at all, and wish to give up even food and drink, and nourish not, but starve to death, this ever-yawning, all-devouring I.

"This Mind that makes such willing slaves of us, and flings us ceaselessly from place to place, itself not resting for a single moment in the heart—I have no wish to serve this tyrant any more, and yet know not how to subdue its giant strength. Easy it were to drink the ocean; easier to pluck the whole of the Mount Meru by the roots; far easier to eat the flames of fire; it is not easy to restrain the mind.

"And stronger than the mind is Trishna([1]). Burning quenchlessly within, it consumes me as the sun's glare kills the morning's moistures. The highest reaches of perfection, whereon I try to give my faith a resting place, it undermines and tumbles down like some strong-toothed burrower of the earth. Like dead leaves in the swirl of the waters; like light straws in the sweep of the storm; like pale clouds in the skies of autumn; helplessly I whirl

(1) Desire; literally thirst; the will to live.

about in the race-grounds of Desire. I have only heard the wonder that the wise cut through its adamantine firmness with the flawless sabre of Viveka (1). But yet it seems to me that even the edge of the sword, or the spark from the forge of iron, or even the tongue of the lightning, is not so strong and keen as the Trishna that rules in the heart.

"See further wherein this strong Trishna centres! This foul frame of flesh and blood and bone that is so dear to us! Its very being is pretence and falsehood! Unknowing in its nature, yet it knows; composed of many, yet appearing one; foul everywhere and yet seeming so fair; it is not dead, nor is it yet alive. I have no love for this old house of mine, an open thoroughfare for ceaseless winds, o'erspread with cobwebs feigning shape of nerves, running with filthy drains in all its parts, painted with blood, plastered with things impure, raftered with bones belonging to the burning place by right and only borrowed thence for a brief while, and undermined withal and shaken by the legion vermin of disease. O Muni!, I would leave it and go forth before it falls about me of itself. I do not under-

(1) Discrimination—between the real and the not-real, the Self and the not-Self, the Eternal and the Transient.

stand why men should love this false and faithless friend that follows not one step to help the soul when it sets forth on its last long lonely and lightless way, though this same soul did nurse and nourish it so lovingly, so carefully, day after day, even from infancy unto old age. False friend !, it is our friend only so long as we provide it with good meats and drinks ! I will have naught to do with it, or wealth or kingship or desires. But a few days and Time shall sweep them all away.

" When I go over silently in mind the various stages in the life of this unstable frame of ours, my love for it is lost without return. Think of the helplessness, the ailments and the thirst, the dumbness, non-intelligence and greed and restlessness and piteousness of infancy, its fits of crying, cruelty and rage. It seems to me that not in later life, in youth or manhood or old age, are our sensations and our cares so keen as during child-hood. A life of ceaseless terror is the child's, and of restraint from parents, teachers, and from elder children, and ever are its wishes thwarted everywhere. They are not wise that say childhood is happy.

" Passing beyond the ills of infancy, the human being rises into youth only to fall again. The lusts of life then take firm hold of him and, helpless as the child put into trance with the black crystal, he obeys their inspirations. Smiling for a brief moment like the lightning, only too surely youth precedes the groans of thunder and the tears of rain. Burning and sweet and bitter all in one; stained with sore sin, yet varnishing its vice and hiding it under the paint of beauty; this passing flush of youth, like flush of wine, it has no charm for me. Unstaying, like the city of the sands; more evanescent and more weird than dreams; hollow at heart like mercenary loves; headstrong, muddy, and uncontrollable, like shallow streams, swollen by slightest showers—such is the youth bepraised by paltry wits. The reason that is rightest runs to wrong beneath its sway. In its mad reign the mind that is most pure, most placid and most self-contained, o'erbreaks its bounds, and grows tumultuous and turbid and discoloured, even as waters in the rains, however transparent they had been before. Youth is a spreading forest, wherein dwells at ease and roams at will the mighty elephant of Abhimana [1], and the snakes of sin infest the tangled undergrowths of the mind's fancies in its depths.

(1) Pride, arising from the sense of separateness which leads to a feeling of superiority over others.

Youth is a lotus flower, pollened with sensations that pall in the tasting, petalled with evil pranks that lead to pain, beloved of the black bees of remorse and care. Youth is an ocean, surging with the countless waves of vice, amongst which there disport the myriad sharks of ailments bodily and mental. More, far more difficult is it to cross unwrecked this ocean, than the other ocean of mere waters with all its storms and tempests and mischances. They are the happy, they are the blessed, they are the Great Ones to be worshipped, who have passed beyond its turmoils safely into Peace.

"They say that Love is glorious. Alas! the short-lived loves of youth and sex, between these dolls of flesh that we are, dolls fashioned with a little flesh, moulded over bones, and tied and held in place with thongs! The eyes that see the depths of Heaven in each other—they are but skin and nerves, blood, pigment and salt tears. The flowing locks, perfumed with sweetest scents, the maze of shining curls that dazed the mind, the bloom of burning gold, the moon face and its smiles like blowing lotus buds, the glowing bust down which the wreaths of priceless pearls streamed like the streams of Ganga down the snowy slopes of Himavat and the golden sides of Meru, how are these fit food, O holy

Muni !, for the fire of the cremation ground and its ill-omened birds and beasts of carrion! What is the meaning of these strange and cruel things, O Sage? Alas ! these dazzling limbs are all mere flesh. The ruthless winds shall blow about the ashes of those forms that were erstwhile unto each other the whole concentred world with all its joys.

"And even worse than youth is the old age we see around us. Far better youth should die than pass into the living death of age. As youth did mar the innocence of infancy, so age fitly destroys the joys of youth. As the hot blast dries the dew-drop, as the hoarfrost blights the bloom, as the torrent tears down green trees, so old age o'er-powers youth. No friend remains to help that sure defeat. Even intelligence, at the approach of age, deserts the man, like a high-minded dame insulted with a rival. Only a ceaseless, helpless, craving for the past makes a lasting home in the desolate heart, even as obscene vultures make their roost in old, leafless, and scorched and stunted trees. And ever-present terrors of the future sweep over it as hot winds sweep over the desert. Better to see a city long deserted, better to see a noble tree cut down, better to see a fertile plain parched by long drought; it is not good to see an age-wrecked human frame.

Whom not the mightiest foes could conquer in the field of battle, who pierced an unchecked path through the very mountains; behold how easily they are over-mastered by weak old age. I have not the courage to face it, O Muni!

"I cannot understand how grown up men should hope and try, like little children, to grasp and press sweet tastes from mere glassed images of fruits. Alas! even the false paints of these images, the forms and colours that attract the infant's hand, even they shrink and shrivel up and disappear beneath the burning touch of Time the ruthless. Naught is there in the worlds that Time doth not devour. Truly is it the Ishvara of all Ishvaras, God of all gods. None is beyond its sway. We cannot trace the limits of its vast dominion. We try to comprehend and compass it within a year; but see, it stretches back behind and on before, as the Great Yuga (1); when we calculate the limits of the Yuga, it once more advances and recedes into the Kalpa (2). Whatever there is of the Beautiful, whatever there is of the Good, whatever there is of the Firm and the Weighty, be it Sumeru's (3) self,

(1) Four yugas, or ages, which make up 4,320,000 years.

(2) A kalpa is a thousand yugas, or a "day of Brahma."

(3) Meru, the great mountain, the axis of the earth, the emblem of stability and permanence.

hopeless and helpless it disappears in the ever insatiable maw of Time. The pitiless, the hard, the cruel, the rough, the miserly, the mean—these too are equally good meat for it. Aho! the wondrous perseverance of this Gardener! Ever is he growing all these fruit-like worlds, and ever is he eating them. Countless are the plants, planets and stars and comets, in his garden; Brahmas are their roots; Devas are their branches; the Loka-palas (1) are the insects in the rotten fruits that he delights in. The days are the flowers—each haunted by a night bee—with which he weaves his endless wreaths and chains. The suns and moons and all the orbs of heaven are his playthings, lighter in his hands than balls in the hands of babes.

"Many are his names: Kritanta, the Ender; Daiva, Doom incarnate; Maha-kala, The Great Turner of the Wheel of Countless Cycles. Destiny is his grim bride. Hand in hand they dance an awful dance in celebration of the Kalpa's end. Thrice purchased slaves of theirs are we, and they our masters, all devoid of mercy. Ruthlessly they drive their slaves and prematurely wear them out. Their

(1) The eight Regents of the world, one on guard at each of the four points of the compass and the intermediate points.

ever-oppressing tyranny transforms our foods into unwholesome poison. The world grows only sick with sensuous joys. Wherewith we seek our ease yields but disease. Our own limbs become our enemies. Truth turns to falsehood, and in sheer despair the self destroys itself, unable to endure that great oppression longer.

"Wherein shall we find rest, wherein relief, from this relentless horror of impermanence, of helpless slavery to Change and Time ?

"Ever this stream of living things is vanishing into the shambles of non-entity. Old landmarks disappear ; broad countries change their faces ; the mountains are worn down by ceaseless-flowing waters into mire and marsh and sands and dust. Where we behold today an immense hollow like the dry bed of an ancient ocean, there we see tomorrow a towering mountain crowned with clouds ; where that mountain, clothed in green and spreading forests, lifts its head to-day to greet the skies, there next day stretches a flat and arid plain. The body that today is decked with silks and wreaths and unguents, lies tomorrow in the grave, all bare and wasting into putrid dissolution. Where we see today the busy city restless with its multifarious life, there a few days later reigns, without dispute, the silent wilderness. The man that glows with majesty today and is the sovereign of many lands, becomes but in a few days a heap of fast dispersing dust. Lush vegetation yields its place to sands; lands change to waters, waters into lands. The seas dry up; the earth, the stars, crumble and disappear; the Siddhas [1] die; immortals meet with death; Indra [2] does not escape; and Yama's [3] self, who swayed and ruled all others, falls under another's sway; Brahma [4] the Parameshthi [5], has an end; the unborn Hari [6] too passes away; and Bhava [7], Source of Being, goes himself into Non-Being.

"How then may feeble souls like mine find rest from fear of Death, and Change, and Ending?

"Tell me, O Munis!, how have ye, whom the world calls the Great Ones, sinless Jivan-muktas, Emancipate of Soul while living yet within this prison of flesh, attained to this unshakable calm of spirit? How have those, Janaka and the others, whose story is conveyed to us by rumour and

(1) The 'accomplished', the 'perfected'; superhuman beings who live to the end of a kalpa.
(2) King of the Gods.
(3) God of death.
(4) The Creator.
(5) The Supreme.
(6) Vishnu.
(7) Shiva.

tradition, attained that Peace ? What insight is yours, what secret knowledge, whereby ye are ever in harmony with others and with Self ? How do ye and they walk in the world without being soiled by all its mire and all its foulness ? What great Being, passed beyond Samsara, shall I ever bear in mind to help me as example ? What other way may I pursue assiduously to gain this Peace of mind ? How may I realise my own Eternal Fulness, whereafter I may not suffer from doubts again ?

"Or if no way exists, O Brahmanas !, or if none tell it me though it exists, or if I find it not myself, with laborious search and long, then shall I give up this place of pains wherein so long I have abided, thinking it was my body. It is not mine, nor am I its at all, and like the flame of the lamp unfed with oil, I too shall pass into extinction, being unnourished with desire."

CHAPTER IV

The Promise

So ended Rama's speech to the assembled Rishis, as end the peacock's notes, suddenly exhausted, after welcoming the deep dark rain-clouds, bending laden with the waters of compassion over the faint and thirsty earth.

The Rishis heard that sweet and wondrous speech which was to wash away in its strong flow the stains of many a mind. They heard it with deep joy. The King, his ministers, and chiefs and honoured citizens, heard it in silent wonder. The mothers and the ladies heard it, seated in their gallery windows, in a stillness and an awe in which their very ornaments forgot to tinkle. The birds perched in the garden-creepers and the niches of the palace walls listened, suppressing their own melodies to drink that sweeter music. The wanderers of Heaven heard those words. "Sadhu (1), O Prince !, well done !", the Siddhas cried. And after that, for the fourth part of a Muhurta (2), flowers fell from Heaven over the gathered Sabha (3), like stars down-rushing in their eagerness to hear that high converse, or like approving smiles of heaven's dames sent down in luminous crystals to the earth.

Then the people heard the Siddhas whispering to each other, how they had roamed the heavens for long eons, and never heard from earth discourse like this, which for its restfulness and wisdom was

(1) Excellent.

(2) The thirtieth part of a day-night, or forty-eight minutes.

(3) Assemblage.

not excelled by work of even the Lord of Speech, Brihaspati himself, and which instructed and enlightened even the dwellers of the skies. The Siddhas said : "Most meet it is we hear what the great Rishis will pronounce hereon, for see, Narada, Vyasa, and Pulaha have come already ; let us hasten then and stand around King Dasharatha's court like bees around the blooming lotus."

With this that luminous procession of the Munis streamed into the court of Dasharatha, till all its greatness grew too small for more. The chief of Rishis, Narada, was there, still holding in his hands the sweetly sounding Vina (1). And there beside him sat the Rishi Vyasa, dark with the soft blue darkness of new rain-clouds, and Bhrigu, too, and Angira, Pulastya, Chyavana, Uddalaka, Ushira and Sharaloma—a very clustering of suns enhancing by their contact the glories of each other.

Then in the hall of Dasharatha's palace was seen a sight unusual. As the members of the court rose to their feet to greet the coming Rishis and the Siddhas, the denizens of air mixed with the dwellers of the earth, sceptres, wands of office, implements of sport, mingled with the dandas (2)

(1) A stringed musical instrument.

(2) Sticks çarried by ascetics ; the Sannyasin is an ascetic who has renounced all.

of Sannyasa, braids of hair twisted with durva-grass shone side by side with locks crested with jewelled crowns ; dresses of sacred bark rustled in company with cloth of silk and gold, and rosaries of beads of crystal rested side by side with chaplets of gleaming pearls and jasmine-flowers.

Vasishtha, Vishwamitra, and the king welcomed the august visitors, each and all, with Arghya ([1]) and with Padya ([2]), as required by the old and gracious rules of courtesy, and they too greeted these in turn, and all took seats and turned with praise to Rama.

The Anuchanas—they who know the Scriptures in their full completeness— blessed him and addressed him thus : "Wise are thy words, O Prince !, and full of sweetness. Very rare are they. And often long we wait before we find one of such promise as thou art. Many are the trees that grow luxuriantly and clothe themselves in heavy foliage. Few are the plants of sandal that impart their fragrance to the axe that cuts them down. Many are the dolls of flesh and blood and bone that thou hast spoken of. Not often do we find a true mind

(1) A ceremonial offering of rice, durva-grass, flowers, etc., and water presented to persons of high spiritual rank.

(2) Water for washing the feet.

lighting one. They pass through the old rounds of birth and age and death, of pains and pleasures, and are not yet aroused to think what this Samsara is and means. Few are they that like thee, Rama !, try to take account of what has gone before and what lies after. Few are they whose intellect flames like thine to make light for itself and for all others. But be thou happy. As thy words are full of wisdom, and of the sweetness and the sadness of Vairagya, so do they carry in themselves full hope of happiness and peace. Never have these, Viveka and Vairagya, failed to bring with them Bodha, enlightenment and rest. Twofold is desire; one is the foul, the other is the pure. The one ties to the wheel of births and deaths. The other helps to free the Soul therefrom. The one is dead in thee; the other has now taken large and vigorous birth. And if we cannot show to thee, O Prince !, the light thou seekest, then the very being of the Munis were in vain. Be thou happy, Prince !, for thy enlightenment is near."

[*End of the Vairagya Khanda.*]

BOOK II

THE QUALIFICATIONS OF THOSE WHO DESIRE DELIVERANCE

CHAPTER I

The History of Shuka.

" Like Shuka's history is thine, O Prince ! " said Vishwamitra. " Naught more remains for thee to know. Thou hast thyself with thine own subtle mind found what there is to find. Like a fine mirror it requires but burnishing alone to catch the image of the Truth quite truly. Listen then to the helpful story of Shuka. He was the bright son of the Rishi Vyasa, now sitting here beside thy father. Long did Shuka, sacrifice incarnate, ponder in his heart the mystery of this Samsara, and by himself determined that the world was nothing more than mind. Imagination, active, makes it live ; imagination, ceasing, makes it cease. The Self behind the mind is the Supreme Omnipotent. Shuka saw this Truth, but was not confident ; only his mind stayed steadfastly away from fleeting sense-enjoyments. Once he asked his father, sitting in a silent region of the mountains : 'How does the mirage of Samsara take its rise; how ceases it; and where and when and whose is it?' And Vyasa told him. But he answered: 'I myself thought this.' And still he gained not confidence. Then Vyasa told him: 'Go to Janaka; he knows.' And Shuka went and was announced by the king's warders to the king, saying the son of Vyasa waited at the gates. Then Janaka to try him, only said, 'Let be,' and thought no more of him for seven days. Thereafter he permitted him to come into the courtyard of the palace. There, too, Shuka stayed for seven days awaiting. Then Janaka commanded that he should be led into the inner halls; but he himself would still not see him. So for a further space of seven days Shuka waited, tended by lovely maidens and served with dainty foods and drinks. But Shuka lost not, any time, his calm of mind, nor at the pains and humbling, nor at the honoring and the pleasures, and ever sat silent, and happy, like a moon full and unwaning. Then the king saw him and saluted him and spoke: 'What wishest thou, ascetic youth? Thou hast gained all that there is to be gained, and hast done all that there is to be done!' Shuka replied with his one question: 'Tell me, O teacher!, how this glamour of the world comes into and goes out of being.' And Janaka told him what his father had already said to him.

"Then Shuka: 'So I found myself, with laboured thinking, and so too did my father tell me when I questioned him. You now say the same, and the same is the final finding of the Shastras, viz., that this world arises merely out of the Vikalpa (Imagination) of the Self, and ceases with it; there is no deeper substance or substratum in it. Tell me the truth again, O king! Is it even so? Is it no more than this? Shall I put faith in thee, and take my peace of heart from thee?'

"Janaka said: 'Yea, it is even so. There is no deeper truth than this. There is no other finding. The nearest is the dearest; the deepest is the simplest. The man is Breakless Consciousness alone. And by its own imaginations does that Consciousness place itself in bonds and free itself again therefrom. Thy intelligence, O steadfast youth!, has ceased to take joy in the things of sense, and therefore, turning back, has seen the Truth. Thy father, with all his stores of self-denial and of knowledge, has not attained such fulness of the Truth as thou hast. I am more than thy father, and thou art more than I, in the attenuation of sense-cravings.'

"Then was Shuka satisfied, and sat, all silent, firmly fixed in the Supreme Free of sorrow, free of fear, free of laboured effort, free of wish and free of doubt, he went into the solitudes of Meru later on, for practising Samadhi, and being perfected therein, at the end of a myriad years, he entered into the Atman, even as a tiny drop of water merges into the ocean."

CHAPTER II

The Disciple and the Teacher.

Turning to the gathered Rishis, Vishwamitra continued: "Thus hath Rama also found the Truth. The proof thereof is this—that he takes joy no more in things of sense. For while the mind revolves and revels in them is it bound. Soon as it turns away from them is it emancipate. And this comes not to pass, this turning back, till after manifold frustration of the search for pleasure. Even as the dawning of the day is simultaneous with the passing of the night, so is the dawning of true knowledge simultaneous with the passing of desire. And that which Rama feels within himself already is the Truth, and he requires but confirmation from the lips of some one who has gone before in the same path, to know it so, even as the sun requires support from Time to rise into the perfect strength and glory of noonday. Let Vasishtha give the confirmation needed. He is the ancient teacher of the solar race of Kings. He sees the past, the present and the future, all as present. Dost thou recall to mind, O Sage Vasishtha !, the teaching that the Lotus-Born[1] Himself addressed to thee and me, in far past ages, to quench with its pellucid waters the fire of the great feud between us, and to help all growing souls at the same time, on the pine-crowned summits of Mount Nishadha ? Brahman ! re-utter then that teaching to this most deserving pupil."

To this the Munis, all with one accord, said, " It were well."

Vasishtha then, son of the Lotus-Born, and glorious as his Father, said : " O Muni !, I shall do what thou hast asked of me, for how can I refuse thy wish, a wish that seeks the truest welfare of the sons of Dasharatha. For their sake shall I call to mind again unbrokenly the teaching given us by Svayambhu, the Self-born."

(1) Brahma; the land surface of the earth is like an open lotus inverted over a sphere of water, with the capes as the apices of the petals. The presiding deity, " Collective and vast mind," is said, in Puranic myths, to be born from and seated on this.

CHAPTER III

The Pace of Progress.

Here Rama asked a question of Vasishtha: "How is it that Shuka's father Vyasa, who knows all, has not attained to such Deliverance as his son?"

And he replied: "The swarms of worlds that came into existence in the Past, and passed away, within the Light of the Great Central Sun; the worlds that throng it thickly Now as motes the rays of the sun visible; the worlds again that will be formed and be destroyed in the Future—these may not be counted. The Jivas that are born in them again and yet again, passing through worlds within enwrapping worlds, subtle and subtler, even as the layers of skin that fold successively the heart of the plantain stem, these Jivas are not all or always similar. The Vyasa sitting now beside me is the thirty-second that I can remember. Twelve of them had realised the truth of the Supreme but faintly. Ten were high. The rest were higher still. And in the endless future will be born again, Vasishthas, Vyasas, Valmikis, Bhrigus, Angirasas, and others. So are these many races of Men and Gods and Rishis born and reabsorbed repeatedly. This is the seventy-second Treta of the Kalpa we are in. And the same Treta-Cycle will appear again in other Kalpas. Many are the times we all have been together in the past, as also separately, and so again shall it be in the future. Even as a heap of grain removed from granary to granary ever assumes new order of arrangement, new combination, so do the Jivas in the universe. The man who has attained to inward peace passes unfretting through the rearrangement. So this Vyasa, free of fear and care, but only Jivan-mukta yet, has been born ten times already, and has eight more births before him. In the end he will arrange the scriptures, write the famous story of his race, and then, attaining to the place and office of the Lotus-Born Hiranya-garbha, (1) pass into the Final Peace.

" Difference of kinds in Mukti, as Jivan-mukti and Videha-mukti, is, O Rama !, a fact only when the subject is looked at from without ; to the inner view, Mukti is one and always. The waters of the ocean, sleeping in the windless bays, or heaving in the storm-tossed waves, are only water still. So, too, That which is the Free, is free within the body as without. The outward form of the Muni is mere sense-object, and gives not evidence of the Deliver-

(1) Hiranya-garbha, 'golden womb,' name for Brahma, one of whose forms is the sun.

ance of the Spirit. That is a thing internal, and is more perfect as the effort inwards is more perfect.''

CHAPTER IV

Exertion and Destiny

"Spare not Effort. Think not anything of Fate. All is within the reach of everyone in all this universe, if only due endeavour shall be made, and the seeker turn not back, losing heart half way. By tireless effort only, has one individual Jiva [1] gained the place of Indra, king of the three worlds. By tireless exertion only, has another 'wave of Chit' [2] become the Lotus-seated Brahma, the Creator of these worlds. So by highest efforts of their own have two great Beings gained the foremost places of Vishnu and Mahesha. Indeed, when of two fruits that grow on the same stalk, one gains its true fulness of juice and roundness, while the other hangs sapless, and dry, and hollow, know that this is caused by nothing else than the latent consciousness of Rasa (sap) making due effort in the one alone and not the other.

"Two are the kinds of effort: the effort of the

(1) An embodied, individualised soul.

(2) The Principle of Consciousness.

past and the effort of today. Of these two, the latter will prevail over the former, and well-directed effort will achieve its object, even as light brings out the difference of colours. Man always gets only as he endeavours, and his convergent previous Karma only constitutes his Daiva-Fate. There is no other fate than this. And like two rams they fight, these two, the present Karma and the past, and now the one prevails and now the other, and the stronger wins at last. Therefore let the man call up his energies, and, setting teeth and clenching hands, let him conquer past with present effort. The past may be long gathered, but the present can be carried longer still into the future. The common cry, 'Tis fate!,' of men after defeat, is nothing but the cry, 'Oh! misery!', that men will utter after suffering. It only means the fact that the past evil Karma has prevailed in that one instance. How does it forbid, or make impossible, all future effort?

Then let the man tread under foot relentlessly the thought that his past fate is driving him. It is not stronger than his present feeling of ability to resist. The man who disregards the immediate evidence of his senses, and would put greater faith in baseless inference, surely insists that his two arms are snakes, and struggles violently to free himself from them. Having a present feeling of ability to work contrariwise, how should the man allow himself to say that he is driven helplessly by his old Karma into evil courses? Surely such a man is most unfortunate, and never saw a great example. Let him tread under foot, I say, such weakling thoughts. Let him labour hard to gain deliverance from his bonds. Let him look always on his house of flesh as something that will pass away one day. And let him therefore strenuously avoid the actions and indulgences that mark the beast, and strive to live the life that marks him man. Let him not delay, thinking 'I will do later,' for the chance may not come soon again. Let him associate with the good, and study hard, and let him never fear his labour will be vain, for there are great examples that have gone before him. So shall he free himself from helpless births and deaths, and so attain the endless joy of Peace wherein all things are Equal, yea, One and the Same, which the wise ones say is highest end of human effort."

CHAPTER V

The Meaning of Destiny.

"Then is there no such thing as Destiny, O Sage?" asked Rama. "Is it not true that all the future is already present in the present, that all the present was existent in the past?"

"Yes," said Vasishtha. "And the truth of it is this. All the past, the present and the future are contained in the Being of the Supreme Brahman. That content is Destiny. That inmost Being makes and is the causeness of the cause, and the effectness of the effect. It includes both; not one only. Effort is included in it as much as the result of effort. All Jivas are embedded in that all-embracing, all-pervading, all-containing Being. None can stand apart from It and out of It, and say, 'This, which is something separate from me, compels me from without to do this thing.' That which is the universal, and supports and gives existence to all possible acts, and moods, and substances, cannot be appropriated exclusively and misapplied for the urging of one only of such moods against another of them. It can be urged in support of both the opposing moods equally. All effects are immanent in that Being. The whole of It may be said to be the cause of each and everyone of these effects. It is manifested by an effect, and may be inferred from it, only after the effect has happened. There is no other way open to Jivas of learning the whole of that Totality of causes, before the happening of an effect. Hence Destiny can never be pleaded as prescribing a particular course of action, but only as explaining it after it has been adopted. For all the purposes of life, each particular course of action must and can be determined with reference only to the circumstances surrounding it immediately and making up the situation, in that limited portion of space and time which is within the purview of the individual concerned. The Self is self-impelled and self-directed. None other can compel it. For, were it so, another would be wanted to compel the other, and so endlessly. The true and full import of this will appear when that nature of the Being of the Supreme which constitutes destiny has been fully understood. In the meanwhile, let every one see well, none can dispense with self-exertion. Let him exert himself in any way he likes ; and, indeed, no man will work in any way but that which will conduce to the accomplishment of the desire that is most strong within him. But let him know for sure, and ever bear in mind most firmly, that good comes of good acts, and ill alone of ill.

"Know well that destiny achieveth not its ends without due means. Both are predestined. Effort is the means for human beings. Desire (Vâsanâ) is realised, materialised, in action. Everyone acts only as he most desires. The long-cultivated and intensified desire of past births appears as the Guiding Fate of this life's actions. The action is the desire condensed, the desire is the mind, and the mind is the man. When men say destiny drives them to do a thing, they mean but this, that the sum of their past Karma is so leading them. That fate which they refer to is this sum, which they have made, for the time being, stronger than their present selves by incurring liabilities to it. In the detailed working of the world, the stronger is the fate of the weaker, nothing else. Then let men try unceasingly by well-directed effort to become stronger than their fate. Behold the Rishi Vishwamitra here. By a thousand years of rigid self-control and high austerities he triumphed o'er the fate which gave him a Kshattriya body, and won true Brahmanahood in that same body, so that I myself, between whom and the Rishi there had been a bitter and most cruel war in bygone ages, welcomed him, by order of the Father of the worlds, as a Brahmarshi.

"So should the earnest searcher, when the mood

of grace is on him, take advantage of it to the utmost and promote it; and when the evil mood asserts itself, then let him battle strongly with it as he can. The mood of grace, the pure desire for knowledge and for peace, is with thee now, as blossom of the plant of virtues nursed and fostered with much skilled and wakeful gardening in the past. See that it wither not, but yield thee rightful fruit. Happy art thou that it has come to thee in early youth at length. Let not that youth go by without securing that which will make all the life to come a calm unbroken; and so attend unto the Science of Deliverance that I expound to thee, as it was given of yore to me by Brahma."

CHAPTER VI

The Origin of the Science

"On what occasion was this science delivered to thee, O Sage !, by the Self-born ?" asked Rama.

Vasishtha answered : "From That wherein Rest and Motion are as one, which is the Inextinguishable Light within all Jivas, whose Nature is best named 'Infinite Principle of Consciousness'—from that Being there arose Vishnu in the beginning of this Cosmic System, as a wave arises on the surface of the ocean. Then from the Lotus-Heart of Vishnu, pollened with thick-crowding stars, was born the

Parameshthi, Knower of the Word, of Scripture and of Scripture-meaning, encircled by the Gods and ancient Rishis, Archangels of wisdom and of power. And He sent forth all this creation from within His Mind. In this country of Bharata Varsha (1), in a corner of the continent of Jambu-dvipa, He placed races of men beset with pains and sorrows, mental and physical. Then, beholding all their wretchedness, a great compassion rose within His mind, as in a parent's at the sight of children in distress. Pondering how they might find release, he called into existence the cardinal virtues of Tapas, Dharma, Dana, and Satya (2), and also the holy places of pilgrimage and worship. But He saw again that these were not enough and that Release, that highest happiness which is named Nirvana, cannot come except from perfect knowledge. Then He evolved me from His mind, and I, appearing from somewhere, like small wavelet on the crest of ocean-billow, stood before Him, humble and obedient. He bade me take seat on the northern petal of the Lotus whereon He was resting, and then said: 'My son! let thy mind forsake its Peace for a brief while, and gain experience of Ignorance, Avidya, and its consequence of rest-

(1) i. e. India.

(2) Self-denying self-control; lawful ways of life; charity; truthfulness and wisdom.

lessness.' With this behest in guise of curse, I lost the memory of my pure stainless inner spirit-nature, and gave place in my mind instead to pain and sorrow and disturbance, and the knowlege of Samsara. Then Brahma said to me : 'Ask me, my son ! the remedy for thy pains, and I will tell thee, so that thou wilt be unhappy nevermore.' And I asked of Him and was taught, and then He bade me go, as embodiment of His knowledge, and teach the Jivas of this Bharata Varsha who required such teaching, and were fit to receive it by Vairagya and Vichara. And so I sit in my place while this creation lasts, doing the duty that was given to me.

"And as He sent me forth, so has He sent forth other Rishis too, Sanat-kumara, Narada, and many others. So, when the happy times of Krita-yuga passed away, the times when all were virtuous, and each knew and discharged his duties to all others, then these Rishis made partition of the common earth into many lands and many countries, and appointed kings to rule in them, that ordinances might be well observed, and laws and limits fail not for the want of persons to enforce them. And many sciences, of Smriti and of Yajnya(1), and of other things, for the achieving of Dharma and of Kama,

(1) Laws and Sacrifices.

virtuous ways and the joys of life, were given out by us to them.

"Then as the wheel of time rolled further onwards, and deeper degeneracy came, and men began ever to step beyond the bounds set for them, and gave way more and more to greed and lust, inclemencies of weather, sufferings from heat and cold, rivalry and wars and the subjection of man to man, and the artifice of wealth and property, with its inseparable consequence of poverty, came on them, and distinctions of rich and poor arose, and penal laws and punishments followed, and sovereigns found it more and more impossible to rule their peoples without engaging in wars with other monarchs. And great despondency and weariness came on these kings, and they were like to fail in their great work of government. Then we, the Rishis appointed for this purpose, first unfolded unto them these stores of knowledge, teaching them to understand the nature and the end of all creation, and see their duties and discharge them with the clear eye and strong heart of true insight. And, for the science was first given to kings, it has come down under the name of Rajavidya, Raja-guhya, Science of Kings and King of Sciences, the Royal Secret Doctrine. Thou too shalt learn it, and so fit thyself for thy great duties.

CHAPTER VII

Who may Ask and who may Answer

"Limited is the Vairagya that is born of special cause. Râjasa is it. A touch of pain breeding dislike of that which gave the touch is lost in the next following touch of pleasure. But thine is the unlimited Vairagya that is born without apparent outer cause, born of the inner sight that makes discrimination between the Fleeting and the Everlasting, and with it realises that the Fleeting, that which has an end, however long drawn out, cannot be separated from its Parting and its Pain. That is the Sattvika Vairagya.

"King Arishta-nemi, when old age came to him, went into the woods to make Tapasya (1), placing the people in the charge of his strong son. Long he dwelt in Tapas in the solitudes of the Gandhamadana mountains. Indra, Lord of Heaven, bade his messengers: 'Go unto king Arishta-nemi. Honour him and seat him on my heavenly car and bring him hither, so he may enjoy the glories and the greatness of my realms.' They went with Indra's message to the king. He questioned them. 'Tell

(1) The same as Tapas or austerity.

me first, ye messengers of Indra!, what the joys and sorrows of your realms may be, and then shall I decide whether I ought to go with you or not.' And they answered him : 'The harvesting of pleasures there is in proportion to the seed sown here of acts of merit. Highest virtues lead to highest heaven ; middling ones lead to the middle plane of it ; the common ones to the lowest thereof only. And jealousy is there of the greater ; and ambition too to pass beyond the equals ; and satisfaction also at the sight of others lower. And at the end, when the store of Punya-merit is exhausted, on the aroma of which the soul fed and maintained itself in those high regions, then comes the fall, and the gods die and redescend into this world. Such are the merits, such the drawbacks and defects of Heaven.' The king heard and cried out : 'Go back to Indra. Much do I respect and thank him. Yet tell him from me that I crave not his joys. Take your car away. I am content with this dire Tapas, with the help of which I shall get rid of this impure fleshly abode of mine.' The messengers went back and made report of this to Indra. He was pleased and bade them go again, and this time lead the king to where the Rishi Valmiki dwelt, and pray the Rishi from him to give unto the king that which he wanted, the Final Knowledge.

"Thou too hast seen, O Prince!, as thou didst well describe, that offices howsoever high, places and powers howsoever great, worlds howsoever glorious, lives howsoever far-reaching in space and long-lasting in time, are still as much short of the Infinite and the Supreme as the lowest, meanest, poorest, smallest and most ephemeral; that mere addition of the finite to the finite will not make the Infinite; that the Inner alone is the Inner and the Infinite, ever-present and ever-available if we would only turn our eyes to It; that the Outer is always only the Outer and always within the Inner; and that the Knowledge of the Inner and the Infinite alone can bring satisfaction.

"Knowledge is the only cure of ills. As the small ills of daily life are tided over with the help of petty knowledge, so can this giant all-pervading Ill of Doubt, Despair and Weariness which lies concealed in the heart of all limited life, however high or low, be mastered only with the aid of the Great Knowledge of the Truth of Life and Death.

"Four are the warders standing at the gates within which dwells that knowledge: Shama (Dispassionate calm of mind), Vichara (Reflection), Santosha (Contentment), and Sadhu-samsarga (Association with the Good).

"He who is in the grasp of that great Ill of Doubt, he who possesses the Sattvika Vairagya, he who has the means to satisfy these four gate-keepers of his fitness, or three or two or even one alone of them completely—for service of the one, if well performed, becomes the service of the others too—he can have those gates opened to him.

"And he who has already passed these gates and made acquaintance with the Resident within, he is the person fit to guide others to that Home of Peace.

"Worthy art thou to ask, and I will answer. The way is the Ancient Way of Rational Intelligence. Walk it with me untiringly. None may transcend it. Reason is the guide of all life. It includes all seeing."

CHAPTER VIII

Attainment of True Knowledge

"Believe, O Prince !, that such high knowledge is, and that untiring search by ever stronger thought will bring to it. Were it not so, how many great and good men had succumbed to care and sought surcease of agony in suicide. Reflection shows the way to cure all pains. Let none think lightly then of such reflection. The men who served Vichara faithfully received from it the gift of that true insight which enabled them to look on all the passing process of the world, its loves and hates, its laughter and its tears, its ecstasies and anguish, with an equal mind, cool, feverless, at peace with all. They have viewed this process as a vast drama wherein the one single actor, Self, becoming the countless players and the scenes as well, lands, seas and forests, endlessly rehearses, for his own pastime, all possible experiences of pain and pleasure. They who have not yet found the secret of this view shall suffer till they find it. But when they find it, then shall this journey through Samsara become as voluntary play to them.

"Holding fast this view, the Great Ones, who have gained the lucid mind and seen the Self, roam in the worlds. They grieve not, want not, ask not good or ill. Doing all their duties they do nothing. Pure are their actions, pure their dwelling-places, pure their ways. All violence of struggle, all wrong views, all prejudices, all partialities, cease when the Supreme Self is seen, and then the mind, free of desires, attains the silent, soft, and sweet sereneness of the cloudless midnight moon of autumn.

"But such high mood is not attained without

beholding the Atma-Tattva, without understanding the Oneness and the non-separateness of all things.

"Then let men strive with all their might, through all their life, to see that Atman face to face.

"Riches avail not in that search, nor friends, nor kinsfolk. Motion of hands or feet avails not, nor torture of the body, nor travellings, nor holy places. Only by conquering the unrest of the mind, by one-pointed Vichara, helped by Shama and Santosha and Sat-sanga, may cognition of the Self be gained, and then by Yoga gradually comes the mergence in it by attenuation of Upadhis. The former may be gained sitting or standing, moving or resting still, by man or god, or Rakshasa or Daitya or Danava, whoever will make Vichara manfully and single-heartedly for it. Indra sought and gained it. Indra's great rivals, Prahrada (1) and his grandson Bali, both mighty monarchs of the Daitya race, did also gain it. So did Vibhishana and others of the Rakshasas. Doubtless that cognition may be gained by any who will really turn to look for it; for the Self is verily everywhere and always, therefore Here and Now.

Thou too, if thou searchest with the help of those four helpful friends, shalt certainly achieve it, and

(1) The same as Prahlada.

be happy as the Jivan-muktas (1)—Hari and Hara and the great Brahmarshis."

CHAPTER IX

Shama and the other Means

" Shama (2) leads to that high knowledge, and is itself in turn perfected by it. Shama is indeed the Final Peace wherein there is no error. They in whose hearts has bloomed the lotus flower of Shama, they have indeed two lotus hearts, like Hari's self. The wealth of the three worlds wins not such joys as ever wait on him who owns the wealth of Shama. The moon in all his glory gladdens not the hearts of men as does the sight of him who has attained to perfect gentleness and is at peace with all his fellow-beings. The enemies of such forget their enmity at sight of him and turn into friends. Even the outcasts, even the abandoned, even the thieves and murderers that may not trust another of their kind, place faith implicitly in such a one when he approaches them. Even as the beast of prey and bird of innocence, good and bad alike, have trust unquestioning in the mother, so even

(1) The Yoga Vasishtha seems to use this word generally as including all the stages of Mukti in which an Upadhi, a material sheath or vehicle, however refined, is maintained.
(2) Tranquillity, calmness non-restlessness of mind.

have all men, of crooked ways or straight, trust suspicionless in him. The very beasts cease from their mutual struggles in his presence. And men take greater joy to see him than they do to see whatever else is dearer to them even than their lives, and they approve with welcome whatsoever he does, with quiet, unelated, unaggressive mind.

He who suffers not from violent elation or depression of the mind, he is the Shanta (Peaceful). He who looks with equal eye on all, and grasps not eagerly or flings away anything, he is the Shanta. He who touches all affairs with an intelligence refined and pure, and ever seeks the good of all and shrinks from causing pain, he is the Shanta. He who does with wakefulness the duties of his life externally, but ever slumbers dreamlessly within, he is the Shanta. He whose glance is ever a glance of tender affection, whatsoever it falls on, he is the Shanta. He whose mind maintains a calm unruffled, through feast and revel as through war and death; who yields not place in his mind for a moment to a mean wish even in dire misfortune, in world-cataclysms, whose mind is ever stainless as the Akasha is although it holds all worlds, he is the Shanta.

"The mind of such a one evolves and radiates around peace from within itself as the stars radiate light. In such a one the Supreme Essence manifests Itself of its own gladness.

" Santosha, deep contentment, is but the fuller and more positive form of Shama.

"Then, purified in mind with Quiet and Contentment, enter thou, O Prince !, on the enquiry into the nature of That which will explain all else, on the Vichara [1] to which thou hast thyself already in thy questionings given form, thus, 'Who am I, and whence; and what and whence is This?' None should despise Vichara. It is man's only refuge, his only instrument of work. All this multifarious life of men is based on nothing else than their Vichara, and all its complex business is conducted by its help alone, though it be righteous now and wrongful then. They seek the remedies for their pains by means of it alone, finding it if the Vichara happens to be deep sufficiently, and failing otherwise. Let none pretend that he can do without Vichara. No more can he do so than he can see with others' eyes, or run away from his own shadow. Even the uselessness or non-existence of Vichara may not be decided except by means of that Vichara. Better the rock-bound toad, better the crawling earthworm, better

(1) Etymologically, the word means 'exploration;' enquiry, reflection, pondering, looking before and after, thinking.

the blind cave-serpent, than the man without Vichara. Only the intelligence that has been sharpened and made subtle by Vichara sees that Highest Being that is subtler than the subtlest.

"Strengthen and make perfect this Vichara by association with the Good Ones. Where they are, emptiness is fullness, ill fortune is good fortune, death is a feast. Their presence is as the searing snow to the poison-plants of evil, as the strong wind to the fogs and mists of ignorance and perplexity. It is as the gentle fostering sun and rain and air to the seeds and the shoots of knowledge. It is enough that they exist on the earth ; more is not wanted.

"Bear in mind, O Prince !, that the greatest gain is the gain of contentment ; that the truest way is the way of the Good Ones ; that the Final Knowledge is the Knowledge gained by deep Reflection, and that the highest happiness is the Happiness of Peace."

[*End of the Mumukshu-Vyavahara-Prakarana*]

BOOK III

THE WORLD-ILLUSION AND THE REAL SELF

CHAPTER I

The Nature of the Drishya (1)

Vasishtha said: "Thou shalt hereafter see fully from what I said to thee, O Prince!, that Shama (2) before Knowledge is the Shama of brotherhood in suffering and sadness; of tender sympathy and love and pity for all things having life, whose common lot is pain; of sympathy, which is the Self's instinctive knowledge of its Oneness with all other selves; or, in another view, it is that utter emptiness of heart from which all living interest in things, all motives for deed of either good or ill, have vanished. The Shama after Knowledge is the Shama of Unity in joy and peace; of Love for all cognised and realised as one with Self; of sympathy, no more instinctive only, but perforce necessitated by perfected

(1) The Seen, the Object-world, as contra-distinguished from the Drashta, the Seer, the Subject.

(2) Self-control.

reason; it is the utter Fullness wherein all being included, there is left, again, no motive for deed of either good or ill, for all is seen as Pastime.

"So too, Right Conduct, Sadachara, before Knowledge, is the inability to add more suffering by one's own selfishness, to the suffering of others, because of that instinctive sympathy. After Knowledge it is the inability to cause pain to the Self now known as one with all selves, because also of utter absence of all motive for exercise of one's own will, as something separate, in manner at all different from the Great Plan of the Creator.

"To gain this peace of mind learn the true nature of Bondage and Deliverance. Samsara (1) is divided into two great halves, Knower and Known, Desirer and Desired, Actor and Acted-on. Pleasures and pains arise from intermixtures of these two. The existence of the Known is the bondage of the Knower. Its non-existence is the true deliverance of the latter. So long as the Seer believes that the Seen is real and independent of the Seer, so long shall the Seer's pains and pleasures too be real. Understand that the object-world is all illusive; thou shalt then understand that the subject-world of endless experiences, painful and pleasureable, is also all illusive.

(1) The manifested universe, the world-process; etymologically, 'that which is moving perpetually.'

Realise that the object-world is not, is naught, and not independently of the Self; thou shalt then also realise that pains and pleasures are not, and not imposed on thee by anything outside thyself.

"How then may the Seen cease to be? If it exists, how can it ever pass out of existence? And if it has no being in reality, how came it then into existence? We see that the Seen is, palpable. It is not wholly non-existent. Also it is always disappearing. From existence it passes into non-existence, and from the latter it emerges back into the former. They say that the non-existent has no existence, and the existent no non-existence. Yet everywhere around us we see this assumed law broken every moment, for change, every change, is a coming into existence of something that was not, and a passing out of existence of something that was. We also see that not until the Seen ceases can we have peace. And yet it is not enough at all to say that the Seen 'is not, is not.'

"Not even by Nirvikalpa-Samadhi [1] can it be effaced entirely. For the most rock-like Nirvikalpa-Samadhi has an end, as is well-known to all who

(1) Meditation when there are no mental images remaining. The man reaches union with the formless Brahman, and naught remains but peace.

have experience of it. And then the Seen wakes up again at the same time as the Seer. For the true seed and source of the Seen is the Nature of the Seer himself. As a small mirror holds within its narrow limits yojana [1] after yojana of mountain, forest and ocean, so does the subtle Self hold all the universe of the Seen within itself. As taste lies hidden in edibles, as oil in the grain of sesamum, as scents in the hearts of flowers, so lies the Seen concealed in the being of the Seer.

"Not by mere denials may the Seen be abolished, not by any mere turning away of the face from it; but by the resolute facing of it, and the grasping of its true nature, may it be rendered powerless to oppress the Seer. Not by tightly shutting the eyes may the child escape from the fear of the phantom, but by looking at it with a light, and understanding that it is something bred by its own foolish fancy.

"This gigantic phantom of Samsara troubles them no more who have examined it with the light of Vichara. [2]

(1) A measure of length, about eight miles.

(2) Reflection.

CHAPTER II

The Story of the Space-born

" Hear thou the story of the Space-born.

" Somewhere there dwells a Brahmana named Akasha-ja (Space-born). Ever intent is he on meditation for the good of all beings. He had lived thus so long that Mrityu (Death) grew jealous, and thought to himself, ' All creations I o'erpower and devour resistlessly. Why do I not thus with this Space-born Brahmana? My power is blunted against him as the edge of the keenest sword on the face of the rock.' And so he went against him once again. He met a wall of fire surrounding his abode. With difficulty he broke through it, and beheld the Brahmana and endeavoured to grasp him with his hundred hands; but failed, even as one fails with physical hands to seize a thing of fancy.

"Then Mrityu went to his lord and master Yama, and asked him why, and Yama spoke: ' Thou art unable by thy self, O Death! to master any living thing. It is the actions of thy prey that make him fall into thy ruthless hands. Go thou then again and seek for those acts of this Brahmana that shall help thee to defeat him.' (1) And Mrityu wandered long through distant countries, lakes, rivers, and forests, mountains, seas, and shores, and towns, and cities, searching for those acts, but never found he any. Then he came again to Yama in his helplessness, and asked him where those acts lay hidden. Yama pondered long and then replied: 'O Death! the Brahmana born of Space has done no acts. Out of pure Space alone he took his birth and therefore is not different from that Space (2). No karma lies behind him, nor is he making any now. No limitations, no desires are there in his nature to manifest themselves in any action, and to be seized upon by thee and broken through. That we see the play of life-vibrations (Prana-spanda) in him is the fault of our own eyes. It is as if all possible infinite shapes and figures that lie embedded in the vast rock of Consciousness—and could be carved as separate statues out of and apart from it, if such an out of and apart from it were possible—should, each of them,

(1) Acts are due to desires and cause changes; desires mean limitations of the self, and limitations necessarily imply a beginning and an end, hence subordination to death, which is only change in excelsis. Wherever there is change death has sway, and men by acting, become subject to death.

(2) The Self, being a plenum, not a void, contains all possibilities that can become actualities. The ideation, by the self, of things as co-existing, is Space. Its thought of them as successive, is Time. The two, as manifested inseparably in Motion, Action, Change, Causation, are conditions of our thinking, feeling, wishing, acting, of existing, in short, as separate individuals, who all live in the Self.

imagine itself as having an existence separate from and independent of that rock. But he whom thou art vainly jealous of, O Death !, doth ever hold to his indentity with the Supreme, and so may not be singled out and separated and attacked by thee. A Being that arises from its Cause without the help of instruments can in no way be different from that Cause. And so this Brahmana, born of Space alone, and one with it, falls not within thy sway, unless he should, of his own wish, harbour thought of death. Thou must perforce confine thy operations to those that join themselves to limitations, thinking, 'I am this piece of earth, this mass of matter, or this, or this.'

'But tell me, Master! how may there be any birth from Vacancy alone? How are, or are not, earth, and air, and fire, and all the others?' So Death asked of Yama, and he made answer:

'He is not born at all, never was He unborn, nor ever shall cease to be (1). All possible things are but parts of His consciousness, downwards from that mountain of Light (2), which to our sight first arises after the sleep of Maha-pralaya. And as a part

(1) He is but the manifested Mind of the Logos out-breathed and in-breathed but never beginning nor ceasing to be.

(2) The Fire-mist, nebulous mass of radiant matter, the central sun of any particular cosmic system of any grade.

may not overpower the whole, so canst thou not conquer Him.'

Mrityu heard this with surprise and smileless went to his abode."

Rama said : "It seems to me, O Sage !, that thou hast been describing unto me Brahma Himself, the Great Father of all things, the Cosmic Mind, the Self-born and the Unborn."

"Truly so, O Rama !, and about Him Mrityu disputed with Yama at the end of a Manvantara, and was thus instructed by him.

"As the castle in the air, as the city of dream-fancies, so verily is all the Seen. The Seer and the Seen have no true being of their own, apart from the being of Param-atma. Imagination is the Mind and the Mind is Brahma."

CHAPTER III

Recurring Questions

Rama asked : "Tell me clearly, O Sage !, what the form is of the Mind from which these chains of worlds are spun."

Vasishtha : "It has no form, O Rama !, Even like space is it, everywhere yet nowhere. Naught else is it than consciousness of an object. It is Samkalpa. Avidya, Samsriti, Chitta, Manas, Bandha, Mala, Tamas,(1) are synonyms of the Seen, and the forms of the Seen are the forms of the Mind; it has no other form of its own. And this, the universe of the Seen, is all within the Infinite Point, the Great Atom of Consciousness (Maha-chit-param-anu), even as light is in the fire, as motion in the wind, as liquidity in the water.

"The state of non-seer-ness which comes to the Seer on the disappearance of the Seen—that is the state of Oneness (Kevali-bhava). When that has been attained, then all desires of Like and of Dislike (Raga and Dvesha) vanish at once, as restless motions from the leaves of the forest when the storm is hushed."

Rama: "But how may the Seen cease to be? If it really is, it cannot lose itself. And that it is not non-existent, our senses testify."

Vasishtha: "Truly is it a startling statement that the world (jagat), and all its 'I am this,' and 'I am this,' has no real meaning. Yet I make it, and I shall try to make it clear to thee, and show that all this that thou seest is nothing else than

(1) Error, Movement, Particularised (Ego-ised) Consciousness, Mind, Bondage, Stain, Inertia.

Brahm [1] ; that that which is already Full expands within its Fullness as it were; that Peace remains in Peace; that Space appears in Space, and Brahm in Brahm ; that in reality there is no Seen, no Seeing and no Seer; nor life nor lifelessness; but only one Great Shanti, everlasting Peace."

Rama : " Thy words, O Sage! are but as if thou saidst—the son of the childless woman has ground a mountain into dust, or that a dead rock is dancing with its arms extended, or that statues of stone are reading, or painted clouds are roaring. What is the meaning of thy saying that this world, with all its solid lands and mountains spreading wide and standing high in space, with all its pains of birth and death, is naught?"

Vasishtha: " What I mean is this: that it is all the creation of the mind, which, while non-existent in very truth, falsely appears as existent."

Rama: " But whence then came this mind and how does it appear as existent when it is not really so?"

Vasishtha: " From That which remains behind in the general dissolutions of Maha-pralayas, the Eternal Being whom words cannot describe adequately, who

(1) The Vast, the Infinite.

is indicated by such names as Param-atma, the Supreme-Self, whom the Sankhya calls the Purusha the Sleeper in the Body, who is the Brahm of the Vedantins, the Vijnyana (Partless Consciousness) of the Vijnyana-vadins, the Shunya-Vacuum of the Shunya-vadins, from whom all this arises, in whom it all has mergence, from whom the gods, Vishnu, and Hara and Brahma, issue as rays from the sun, That from which Time and Space and the ordered Movement of Destiny take their existence, That which transcends all existence. Pure Consciousness, Manas, Thought, or Jnyana, is His sole high and mysterious power. And as jnyana is his nature, so by jnyana only may He be seen and known. Tapas, self-denial, or Dana, charity, or Vrata, fasts and vows and vigils, give no help herein directly."

Rama : "Where may we find and how may we approach this God of gods ?"

Vasishtha : "He is not far to seek. He is in our bodies even. He is all around them. He is they. He is the Universe. Wherever Consciousness is, there is He. Chit—the Principle of Consciousness—is all. Chit is the Wearer of the Moon (Shiva-Space). Chit is the Lord of the Eagle (Vishu-Time). Chit is the Lotus-born (Brahma-Motion). Chit is He that shines, the Sun with the myriad rays."

Rama : "But in this land of ours, O Sage !, we hear this as a commonplace from even the lips of children, and but too often it conveys no meaning."

Vasishtha : "The deepest sayings of the wise become the commonplaces of the people. As I have told thee once, the deepest is the simplest, and the very simpleness of profound truths hides their full meaning, and their all-pervading presence does itself lead to ignoring of them. Try to understand the meaning of the commonplace. A truth is commonplace only to minds that are themselves but commonplace. Yet more, if remedies are commonplace, are not the griefs and ailments, for which these remedies are sought, as commonplace ? The truth is, when the malady is strong, the patient will belittle the medicine applied if it effects not cure within a moment. But persist in the ministrance, and the former loses what the latter gains in strength. If thou shalt try to understand sincerely what Chit may be without an object different from itself, then shalt thou see what frees thee from all pains. Then breaks the bond of the heart, then all doubts disappear, then karmas fall away, for the Final has been seen."

Rama : "Describe again to me, O Sage !, the form and nature of the Final Being."

Vasishtha: "Whatever the form is of Consciousness during its flight, when it rushes from point to point across the most measureless distances, that is the form of the Param-atma (1). That fathomless Ocean of Consciousness wherein the ever-limited world is ever denied (2), is lost, is naught, that is the nature of Param-atma; wherein the complex relations of Seer and Seen, appearing to be, are yet in reality not, wherein are all these crowded worlds but which is empty still, which though composed of Chit is yet like a vast dead rock—such are the Form and the Nature of that Param-atma."

Rama: "How may I understand that that Param-atman is, and that these worlds are not?"

Vasishtha: "He who understands that the world is an illusion, just as much as the colour of blue which appears to belong to the emptiness of space is an illusion, he has in truth understood the nature of the Supreme."

Rama: "Thy words, O Sage!, are as if one

(1) It is the Omnipresence of the Self which alone renders the appearance, the illusion, of flight possible.

(2) The Nature, the Form, the Essence, the Character, the Sva-bhava, the Prakriti, (as we may like to call it), of the Principle of Consciousness, Universal Consciousness, the Supreme Self (which is and includes all individualised, particularised, singularised, embodied, ensheathed selves), is "I-This-Not", an eternal denial by the I of being other-than I. See *The Science of Peace*.

should say that the Mountain of Meru lay contained in a grain of mustard. How may I create within myself the belief that all this solid world is non-existent ?"

Vasishtha : "By long continued stress of thought has this solidity thou speakest of arisen. And as it has arisen, so also and so only may it disappear, as it has disappeared for those we know as Jivan-muktas and Videha-muktas. Surely thou believest that such are ?"

Rama : "Tell me the character of each, O Brahmana !"

Vasishtha : "He who has seen and understood the heart of things, while yet in the body, he is the Jivan-mukta. His face changes never its sereneness, though good befall or ill. Aham-kara, egoism is dead within him. His Buddhi, Reason is not bound to any object by the bonds of Desire. Acting, in performance of his duties, as they act who are moved by the world's loves and hates, he harbours not these roots of all the emotions in his heart of hearts. And when his body (sthula or sukshma or karana, gross, subtle, or causal) falls away in course of time, as his Prarabdha-karma is exhausted, then he enters the condition of the Videha-mukta. The Videha-mukta rises not nor sets. He neither is, nor is not. He is not I ; he is not thou. He shines in the Sun. He rules over the world as Vishnu. He dissolves them as Hara. He creates them anew as Brahma. As ether and as air, he supports the Rishis, Gods, and Titans. He is the Family of Mountains, on the summits of which stand the cities of the Lokapalas. As the Earth too he bears these races of living beings on his broad breast ; as grasses, as groves, and as creepers, he gives forth the seeds and fruits that nourish. Whatever, indeed, appears, he becomes all that."

Rama : "But if the Videha-mukta becomes the three worlds, where is his emancipation from Samsara ? Is he not fallen deeper still into that Samsara ?"

Vasishtha : "It would be so only if that Samsara had true existence, and if the Videha-mukta had not realised that it has no true existence."

Rama : "But how, again, may its non-entity be realised ?"

Vasishtha : "The way uphill is no less long than the way downhill. By patient unremitting effort may this end be gained. Think on the nature of the Seen and of the Seer. What seems so solid today, is it as solid to-morrow ? Hast thou not thyself so well described how seas dry up, mountains crumble away, whole worlds vanish from the painted sheets of space? And does not even common reason say that what is, cannot also not be, that what is not, cannot be? Does it not follow hence that whatsoever undergoes a change is really false, really illusive, has no true existence?

"That only which persists through Maha-pralayas has true existence."

Rama: "This that remains behind after such Pralayas must be formless. On this point I have no doubt. But how should it not then be utter emptiness, mere nothing. Where neither Seer is nor Seen, cannot be else than nothing."

Vasishtha: "Truly a Nothing, but which holds all things within itself. As the marble-block contains within itself all possible shapes that might be chiselled out of it; as the smooth surface of the ocean hides within itself all possible billows that might rise on it, so does the Being that remains through Pralayas contain within itself all possible forms of all Samsaras. The marble figures and the ocean-waves—what are they? Mere modifications of the substance of the marble or the water, modifications, movements, limitations in Time and Space. If, by a great effort of the Buddhi, Motion and Time and Space could be cast out of the illustration, then would it become plain how emptiness and nothingness is full with all existence."

Rama : "Where does the phantasm of Samsara go during these Pralayas ?"

Vasishtha : " Do thou tell me whence arise and where retire the castles of imagination that thou buildest."

Rama : " Still these castles of imagination have a temporary being. They arise and disappear. That should be explained. Allowing even that Samsara has no true existence, still it has a false existence; not absolutely Asat (1) is it, though not all Sat (2) ; at most it shows both aspects, Sat as well as Asat. It is Sad-asat. This leaves behind the ever recurring question : Whence does it arise, whereinto disappear, why does it arise, why end ; why should the Param-atma, Being beyond wants, Being self-complete, eternal Fullness which should be beyond the need for change, ever be casting forth and reabsorbing from and into Itself this hopeless tangle of joys and miseries."

" Brahm is all, Brahm is everywhere, thou sayest. All Jivas should be Brahm if this were so. Yet every Jiva is different from every other. One sorrows here,

(1) Not-Being.
(2) Being.

and one rejoices there, a third looks on indifferent. All Jivas act not uniformly, are not moved by the same motives at the same time. And even were it so, how could those be one which we behold as two, as many, standing side by side and all apart from one another, or indeed moving different ways?"

Vasishtha: "Well sayest thou, O Prince!, such is indeed the ever recurring question. This is the one main point round which all the doubts and the difficulties of the searcher cluster. While it remains unsolved nothing is solved. To tread the path of Truth without an answer to that question is more difficult than to tread one's way without a lamp through a dense forest on a cloudy night. Doubts laid to rest by means other than of such answer, rise again and yet again, like well-armed foes that are only stunned and slightly wounded and not slain. This most helpful answer thou shalt find, O Rama!, if thou thinkest deeply on the true nature of Time, and Space, and Change.

"Thy question tacitly assumes the truth of these, as I indicated even now.

"That one Being should cast forth another or others from Itself, and re-absorb these back into Itself —this Change implies both Time and Space. If Time and Space were not, such change and such succession could not be, nor would there be the co-existence of the Many. If thou couldst see that the Supreme works not in Time and Space, but that both these are in Its Being, then would thy question have been answered finally ; then would the doubt vanish for evermore ; then shouldst thou see that all the changeful process of Samsara is a frozen dream, a changeless vision in the changelessness of the Eternal.

"I shall try to make this clear to thee."

CHAPTER IV

The Story of Lila

[NOTE :—The very instructive, but also at times very obscure, story which is here given, can scarcely be followed without a few hints.

First, it must be understood that a "universe" exists only in relation to those who belong to it, *i.e.*, to those who, being formed of the same materials as itself, are able to respond to the vibrations of which it consists. To them the universe is "existent" and has "form". To all others it is "non-existent" and "formless." Universes interpenetrate each other, but each is "enclosed" from all others by virtue of the limitations of the percipient beings belonging to them. As all of the physical universe that a man perceives is enclosed in the small space of his eye, so is the whole physical universe enclosed within the eye of percipiency common to all conciousness related to it. The universe of the astral plane exists and has form for the inhabitants of that plane ; to them the universes of the physical and mental planes are non-existent and formless. So with each plane in relation to the others. By the highly developed inhabitant of the higher manasic levels the different planes can be called into visibility, and then the physical plane, by reason of its limitations, appears as the smallest and most restricted, a mere "corner" of the vast thought-universe.

Secondly, the universe consists of thought-stuff, Akasha, of vibrations of consciousness. It is the idea of its Logos—nothing more. All types of matter are modifications of the Akasha, and consist of slower and smaller vibrations of it in a descending series.

Thirdly, Time and Space represent the conditions imposed on our consciousness by the Logos. If he is thinking ideas in succession, we are conscious of time and see evolution; when He thinks of the whole simultaneously, the worlds roll up, and time is not. We measure time externally by the response of consciousness to the slow and small vibrations that impress us as "physical matter," but when we change our perceptive capacity, time changes with it, *e.g.*, we may experience years of astral consciousness in a moment of physical time.

Fourthly, according to our perception so is our sense of "reality;" that is "real" to us to which our conciousness at the moment is responding.

These general ideas must be kept in mind in reading the story of Padma and Lila, as a knowledge of them is taken for granted throughout. The life-story is on three planes, the physical, the astral and the mental. The opening scenes are on the astral, whereon have been built, by the action of desire in a previous physical state, all the fair surroundings of the joyous existence of Padma and Lila. The story opens in "Summer Land," and Padma and Lila are in full enjoyment of the astral life, surcharged with passionate emotions, tasting all the delights longed for by Vasishtha and Arundhati—their former selves—on earth.

Additional notes in brackets are added through the story as hints to the careful student to guide him through the intricacies of the maze.—A. B.]

Vasistha said : Listen to the tale of Lila, Prince!

There reigned once on the earth a king bearing the name of Padma. Lila was his queen. Great was the love between them. In parks and forests, groves and leafy arbours, beds of flowers and houses made of tender creepers, in royal palaces and artificial lakes, on mountains covered with the sandal-plant and full of the voice of the cuckoo, amid dark woodlands, and in open glades, amid smiling lotus-beds and trees fruit-laden, amongst bright waterfalls and showers of sparkling spray and slabs of crystal, they day after day enhanced their mutual love and happiness with enjoyments tender and refined, with stories, games and riddles, poems, recitations, dramas, scenes of town and country, wreaths of flowers and gems and graceful ornaments, swings made with strings of blooms, journeys by boats, horses and elephants, sports in the water, song and dance and dalliance, and the luxuries of music from the Muraja and the Vina. (1)

Long years passed away in these enjoyments and then a care shadowed the beautiful brows of the queen. "Dearer to me than life is my husband," so she thought. "How may he become immortal? How may I remain for ever with him? So shall I endeavour, with Japa and with Tapas (2),

(1) Indian musical instruments.
(2) Repetition of mantras and penance.

that never shall my husband's face fade from my sight."

And she consulted with the aged Brahmanas, aged with knowledge, aged with Tapas, aged with many sciences. One answer only they returned to her with one consent: "All else may be attained, O Lady! A mortal body never may be made immortal."

With aching heart did Lila ponder this. She thought: "If I die before my husband it were well, and I were free from pain. But should he die before me, then shall I do so that his Jiva may not pass out of the limits of this palace."

With this resolve she made Upasana [1] of Saraswati and, unknown to her husband, worshipped her in the ways laid down by the Shastras. By hard austerities and strong self-discipline she pleased the Goddess of Speech and Wisdom, and the Goddess appeared to her and spoke: "I am pleased with thy unbroken Tapas and thy Bhakti [2] to thy husband. Name the boon thou seekest."

Lila answered: "O Mother of the worlds! Thou that dispellest the gloom of the heart as the sun the gloom of the outer world! If Thou art pleased with

(1) Worship.

(2) Devotion.

me, then give me this—that if my husband die before I pass, his Jiva may not quit the limits of this palace. And give me this also, that when I pray to see Thy holy form, I may have sight of it and be not disappointed."

"So be it," said Saraswati, and disappeared.

The wheel of time rolled on and what the queen had feared did come to pass. They brought to her one day that much-loved body of her husband, wounded to death in a great battle with unrighteous kings who had invaded the country wrongfully and been defeated, but at the cost of his own life, by Padma. Sad was the state of Lila on beholding him. Now crying and now silent with despair, like one demented, withering like the Nalini ([1]) flung out of its water basin, fading like the lamp flame fallen from its feeding cup, she came near unto dying too.

Saraswati had pity on her plight, and came and said : "Take thy husband's body, child !, and lay it on a heap of flowers. The flowers shall not fade, nor shall the body. His Jiva shall not pass out of this palace, and he shall rise again to give thee joy."

That rain of tender words revived the dying Lila, as the first showers revive the dying Shaphari ([2])

(1) Lotus.

(2) A kind of small fish.

in the lakes dried by the summer sun. She hastened to obey these orders, and at the middle of night, sitting beside the body, she sought again with her whole soul the feet of the bright Goddess. Saraswati appeared, and Lila asked her: "Where is my husband, Mother? What is he doing? Take me to him. I cannot live without him."

The Goddess said: "My child!, there are three spaces, the Common one, the Chitt-akasha and the Chid-akasha [1]. The last is subtler than the other two. That which thou seekest, being composed of sheaths of Chid-akasha only, can be seen and felt, though non-existent to thy present view, by meditation on that Chid-akasha. That which lies

(1) The common 'outer' space is that which we seem to see with the physical eyes; Chitt-akasha is the 'inner' space 'within the mind', or in which intelligence works; and by Chid-akasha seems to be meant what may be described as 'the principle of space', 'root-space', or 'seed-space', the principle of the possibility of the co-existence of the Many, of countless things, within Universal Consciousness.

[The three spaces are the three worlds, physical, astral and mental; all are formed of mind-stuff, but the third is subtler than the others, and in its nature more akin to that in which the creative consciousness works than are the other two. Padma had passed on to the mental plane, and was ensheathed in the matter of that plane. If Lila would find him she must free herself from the denser matter in which she was herself ensheathed, and then she would become conscious of, because responsive to, his world, and would again be in his presence. She, accordingly, we find in the next chapter, entered into meditation, and left her astral and mental bodies; clothed then in the Karana Shariras she could range the mental plane at will. A. B.]

midway in the passage 'swift as the wink of the eye' of Samvit (1), from one place to another, that is Chid-akasha. If thou canst fix thyself in the contemplation of that to the obliteration of all other ideas, then shalt thou attain without a doubt the state Sarv-atmaka (2), that is the underlying basis of all. This state is not realised except with the total non-existence of this Jagat (3). Thou shalt realise it by my favour."

The Goddess disappeared with this, and Lila passed with ease into the state of Nirvikalpa Samadhi (4). As a bird leaves its cage when the door is opened, she left behind her body and antah-karana (5) and there in the space enclosed by that same palace, she saw her husband seated on a throne high in the midst of thronging chiefs, receiving embassies and messages, directing state affairs and wars and expeditions, listening to Veda-chants and music,

(1) Consciousness.

(2) All-inclusive.

(3) World.

(4) Consciousness whence concrete ideas have vanished. Nirvikalpa Samadhi ordinarily means a state of consciousness in which there is no Kalpana, no particular idea or ideation or object, but only the sense of being; here the expression seems to be used in a relative sense; *i.e.*, particular consciousness ceased so far as the object-world of Lila's 'living' body was concerned, but her Jiva woke up on a subtler plane in a subtler body.

(5) Lower mind.

honouring Rishis, and ordering the building of new forts and cities. She saw in his great court and all about it, old faces, the faces of those she used to see in her other body in the capital of the living Padma. She also saw new faces she had never seen before. She went into the court and wandered about in it; but none present there saw her, even as the inhabitants of a city imagined by one man are not seen by another man.

She saw her king, not of the age of the Padma-body that died, but youthful as at twice eight years. And passing out of the court she saw the light of the noonday sun, and towns and rivers, hills, valleys and mountains, all owning the sway of the king. Later on she saw a sky filled with moon and stars and planets.

Seeing all these things she suffered great perplexity and wondered: "Are they all dead, the citizens of our earthly capital ?." (1)

(1) [Padma is now in Devachan, and has created the world in which he is living. He has peopled it with all the figures of his past, and is living actively his royal life, the astral experiences having by no means extinguished his longings for it. Lila is invisible, for no external habitants of the mental plane affect the devachanic consciousness, the world of which is limited to the forms it can itself produce. Later we shall meet the thought-form of Lila herself as consort of Padma. Lila's perplexity as to the dwellers in Padma's world may be shared by the reader; how far were they "real"? The answer is that they were more "real" than their astral plane or physical plane copies. We never

Then with the help of Saraswati [1] she found herself again in a moment in her palace, and saw all there as it had been before [2]. Hastily she roused her sleeping attendants and bade them summon the ministers, and call together all the king's court as usual in his lifetime. They came, and she saw them all alive, and was much pleased. But her perplexity and wonder grew the greater. "Unaccountable is this Maya," she thought. "Our citizens are there as well as here. And parks, and groves, and hills, too, are there in the very image of these I behold here. Even as scenes exist without as well as within a looking-glass, so it seems creation lies within as well as without the mirror of Chit. Which of the two Sargas [3] is false and

know in the three lower worlds more than the thought-form we create of our friend; how much of our friend animates that thought-form depends on two things—his own stage of development and our power of response to him. The more of him we can answer to, the more of him will vitalise our thought-form, but till we reach the Buddhic plane we cannot know him as he is. Any number of thought-forms may be vitalised by an Ego, as rays of one sun may illumine many vases; as much of his life as the form can contain and transmit shines through it. It has been observed in Devachan that an ego embodied on earth may be working actively in the thought-forms inhabiting the "closed worlds" of many inhabitants of devachan. A. B.]

(1) Prajnyapti-bodhena is the original Samskrit expression. It might also mean "owing to the awaking of knowledge"; but this would have no special significance here, and the commentator follows the other interpretation.

(2) She returned to her mental and astral bodies.

(3) Worlds, creations.

which is real ? I shall ask Saraswati."

And the Goddess of Speech came at her prayer. "O Mother of the worlds !", Lila exclaimed on seeing her, "Thou hast set the laws that guide them ! Why sufferest thou that I should be in such unrest of mind ? The Great Ones cannot bear that the weak and deserving of pity should suffer pain. Tell me, then, which of the two worlds that I have seen and see is false and which is real ?."

Saraswati : "Tell me first, my friend, what thou callest real and what false."

Lila : "As I am sitting here, O Goddess !, and Thou art there, this I think is the real. And that where my husband now is, that is the false, because it is empty and occupies not any time or space."

Saraswati : "Thou wouldst say that that world is a fanciful copy of this ; that this is in some way the cause of that. But how can a false effect flow from a true cause ? Effects are not dissimilar to their causes ; and if this world were the cause of that, then that would partake of the nature of this."

Lila : "But is it not so, Mother !, that effects differ from causes ? The lump of earth can hold no water. But the jar made from that earth will do so."

Saraswati : "An effect which proceeds from a cause with the help of instrumental causes may show some difference from that cause. Say, then, what things of this world were the causes of that other world of thy husband's? It seems to me that all the things of that world were born of the elements belonging to it. If these components had gone there from this world, how would this world be here now? What, too, supposing that this world was the cause of that, could be the other helping causes in such case which would help to make it different from this? The instrumentality that arises even in the absence of other causes is not different from the first cause, *i. e*, belongs to that first cause itself, which is therefore material and efficient as well as instrumental cause. Such is the experience of all." (This identity of all the various kinds of causes in one cause occurs only in the single case of Param-atma).

Lila: "May it be that the memory of my husband took that dense and solid shape? I think that memory was the cause. And this world is the cause of that memory."

Saraswati: "My daughter!, as memory is of the nature of Akasha, so too is what is born of that memory. The world of thy husband, though 'experienced' by thee, was only Akasha. But while thou wast in it, was it not to thee as real as this is now? Didst thou not see that world broad-based in space? Didst thou not see that night succeeded day there even as here?"

Lila: "This world, too, then may be like that world of my husband's, all composed of the Akasha of memory?"

Saraswati: "It is even so. And as that false world of thy husband is to thee, so too is this world to me."

Lila: "Tell me how that formless world [1] of my husband was born out of this."

Saraswati: "There is a world-system somewhere in the measureless expanse of Chid-aksha. In some far corner of that system lies a town nestling midst woods and streams and hills, and in that town there dwelt a Brahmana with his wife. The pair were named Vasishtha and Arundhati, though different from the Rishi and his wife. Once the Brahmana sat on the top of one of the neighbouring hills, and saw the King of the country pass below with a great and gorgeous train on a hunting excursion. He saw all that magnificence, and forthwith rose the thought within his mind: 'Happy is the sovereign. All joys attend on him. How may I attain those joys?' Cherishing

(1) Formless to her now that she had returned to the astral consciousness.

this wish within his mind, but still not deviating from the path of righteousness, the Brahmana passed into old age and thence to death.

" His wife, too, like thee, had sought in vain for immortality for her husband, and failing there, had prayed to me and gained boons like the ones I gave to thee. And thus the Brahmana after death became a glorious King, with broad domains yet all confined within the walls of that small house in the nameless town. His wife, too, bearing not that separation from her husband of her lifetime, cast off her body, and in an Ativahika (1) body went to him as loving rivers go unto the ocean.

" Eight days it is now since their death, and the house and the town are all existing, And yet thou art that wife, O Lila !, and that Brahmana Vasishtha was the Padma thou bemoanest now. One illusion giving birth to others, unreal in reality from the standpoint of the Self, but all too real to the view of those who are within it and within its grasp."

Lila heard in wide-eyed wonder and exclaimed : " O Devi !, Thy words may not be false, and yet how may this be? The Jiva of the Brahmana within

(1) "Ativahika" means composed of those elements which carry onwards (vahanti) the Jiva after the death of the body. But it seems to be used in the text in different places to mean different bodies, correct knowledge about which belongs only to occult science.

the walls of his small house, and we the monarchs of far-stretching lands, forests and mountains! The maddened elephant confined within a grain of rye! The mosquito competing with a host of lions and defeating them! The Meru mountain hid in a speck of pollen and swallowed by mistake by an infant bee! Explain thyself, O Devi!, and bear in thy great patience with the slowness of my weak mind."

Saraswati: " I tell thee no untruth, my daughter! If we ourselves did break the great ordainments, who else would observe them? It is true that the old memory of you both was broken and re-appeared in another form. Even as the things of the waking consciousness become during a dream, so do the things of life become after death. It is true I say that all thy wide dominions are confined within the walls of that small house. In the consciousness of Atma, (1) worlds within worlds lie concealed in each Param-anu (2). Doubt this not!"

(1) The Supreme Self.

(2) Atom. [Every atom retains every experience through which it has passed, *i. e.*, retains the vibratory potency evoked by such experiences; therefore to the Atma as intellect an atom contains in each of its sheaths the worlds in which it has been functioning and these may be seen reflected in, or recreated by it, at any moment. Looked at with astral senses by the Chid-atma, the astral world it has experienced would be seen in it; with mental senses the mental world; and so on. The change of percipient sheath would cause a feeling of transition. A. B.]

Lila: "The Brahmana died eight days ago, Thou sayest, but many years have passed over our heads! How may this be, O Mother?"

Saraswati: "As Space has no real dimension, so Time has none. As all this appearance of an extended Universe is mere Pratibha, mere consciousness, mere imagination, so also the appearance of Time, from a Kshana to a Kalpa (1), is mere Pratibha. And even as in dreams so in the case of dying, the Jiva after passing through the swoon of death, forgets his preceding condition and awakes into a different set of appearances, with different times and spaces. A single night became twelve years to King Harishchandra. Hopes deferred make years of single days."

Lila: "What memory was the cause of the creation wherein the Brahmana and his wife had their home?"

Saraswati: "The memory of Brahma was that cause. The Final Cause is the Idea in the Maha-Chit, the Supreme Consciousness (or Unconsciousness) wherein cause and effect are one." (2)

(1) An instant to an age.

(2) [The Jiva commencing its experiences in the physical life originates in the Divine Idea; "Super-consciousness" would more accurately represent the fact than the pair of opposites, consciousness and unconsciousness. A. B.]

Lila: "Not without much application may this be well understood, O Goddess! In the meanwhile, if thou thinkest fit, take me to the town where the Brahmana and his wife were dwelling."

Saraswati: "Abandon then this body that thou wearest, by resting on the consciousness that has withdrawn itself from all objects."

Lila: "But why may not other worlds be visited in this same body?"

Saraswati: "The formless worlds assume form to the corresponding consciousness. Even the worlds created by the imagination of the man cannot be seen by that same man's physical eye."

Lila: "And shalt thou go there in the same body that thou wearest now?"

Sarasvati: "Yes, for mine is already a Manomaya Deha (mental body) (1). Thou too couldst make one with long practice. Nothing is accomplished without practice."

After this conversation beside the body of

(1) [A Mayavi-rupa, formed at will by the trained will out of mental matter, and capable of being changed and adapted to varying conditions by the same will. A Deva or Devi normally uses such a body, when functioning in the three worlds, but a high Devi, such as Saraswati, would have the Jnyan body spoken of later, and the Manomaya Deha she speaks of would be put forth from it. A.B.]

Padma in the closed room, filled with the fragrance of the flowers on which it was reposing, the two entered into Samadhi, holding their bodies motionless like statues carved in stone. Casting off all consciousness of outer things they retired into themselves like lotus flowers at the end of day, and became motionless like the white clouds resting against a mountain-peak in the absence of the breeze.

Then they rose into space, stretching through endless millions of Yojanas (1), the Goddess in her own old form, and the human in a Jnyan-body (2) suited to that experience.

(Note :—The text summarised in the above chapter is very difficult to follow because in it metaphysic loses its preliminary character of theory, and in combination with psychic matters appears as a practical occult science of which the lay world has no knowledge. This difficulty occurs again and again throughout the text, and the reader should carefully bear in mind that the present English abstract can in no way claim a certainty of accuracy in the summary of these portions, such as it does

(1) A Yojana is about eight miles.

(2) [Knowledge body. A cosmic body formed by the aid of Saraswati. Occult students will recognise its nature from the experiences related, and the hints given in a later note A.B.]

in dealing with the mere descriptive or narrative portions. The reader should himself undertake further research and satisfy himself independently if he is interested in the subject.)

CHAPTER V

The Story of Lila (continued.)

Hand in hand they went, beholding all the wonders of those depths, profound and pure, more shoreless than the swelling ocean, more transparent than the good man's mind. Passing through the zones of clouds illumined by the ceaseless play of the lightning and the atmospheric currents flowing high above, they crossed beyond the orbit of the moon. Then Lila saw new sights and felt all the immensity of space, empty despite its countless millions of orbs. This was the giant pathway of the Gods and the Titans. Siddhas passed them on Vimanas (1), rushing with a whistling sound so dense it could almost be grasped by the hands. Planets and comets speeded by. Yoginis and Dakinis, (2) creatures of strange and monstrous forms, Siddhas and Gandharvas (3) circled around. Here

(1) Heavenly cars.

(2) Ascetics and goblins.

(3) Super-human beings and heavenly musicians.

they beheld the city of the Rudras, there the abode of Brahma. In one part were flaming Suns creating constant day ; in another reigned a darkness dense as the heart of the rock. Now they witnessed great battles between the Devas and the Daityas (1); and again the clash of a hundred comets hurtling together. At times they went through space glowing with quenchless heat; again through parts freezing as mounts of snow.

Passing thus through many scenes of marvel, seeing many worlds with many forms, they came finally to successive enwrapping shells of earth and water, fire and air, and ether, each ten times as large as the preceding, and piercing through them passed beyond the limits of that Brahmanda (2).

Then they came to another world and lighted on the earth that was in the mind of Saraswati (3).

(1) Gods and Titans.

(2) Egg of Brahma, *i.e.*, universe or system, but here used for plane.

(3) [The lesson given to Lila by Sarasvati was of the most instructive character. It is a peculiarity of the Jnyan body that it can function on any plane and a body of the matter of any plane can be evolved from the root of that matter in itself. It appears that a manasic Mayavi Rupa similar to the Manomaya Deha of the Devi was evolved for a flight through space. For in the Mayavi Rupa, subtle as may be the matter of which it is composed, a sense of passing from one place to another, however rapidly, is experienced, while in the Jnyan body itself there is no such sense of motion. "The quenchless heat" experienced in passing near or through a forming incandescent world, and the cold

There they saw, themselves invisible, the house of the Brahmana, its men careworn, women with weeping faces, servants cheerless, painful to see, like flowers with withering petals—all for the recent loss of its head and master.

Then the wish arose in the mind of Lila : "May these folks, so full of sorrow, see the Goddess and myself wearing the ordinary shape of women." And forthwith it was so, and the people of the house thought that they beheld before them Lakshmi and Gauri ; and headed by Jyeshtha, the eldest son of the dead Brahmana, they bent before them and laid flowers at their feet. The two then questioned them why they were all so sad, and Jyeshtha answered : "My parents, who were the heads of this house, have just been taken away by death, and therefore are we sad, and not we only, but the whole village, so good were they to all. Even the creepers in the surrounding woods are restless in their sorrow and make gestures of pain with their leafy hands, and the rivulets of the neighbouring

radiated from a dead one, should be noted. The "enwrapping shells" are appearances caused by different dimensions of space. They had begun their flight amid the archetypal worlds of the upper manasic levels, where the great creative activities are at work, and the wars of the Gods and Titans are waged, and they sped onwards through the lower manasic regions to the astral, dropping finally to the physical plane. A. B.]

hills fling themselves from heights to the rocks below and shatter themselves into a hundred fragments, all for the bitterness of their great loss. Do ye something to relieve our sorrow. Vision of the Great Ones should not go in vain."

Lila touched the son on the head with the palm of her hand and a great peace came over him. The other members of that household, too, forgot their trouble in the joy of seeing these two heavenly forms, and cheerfulness came back once more to that desolate home.

The two then vanished from their view ; and Saraswati asked the wondering Lila : "What more wishest thou to see and know ?"

And Lila asked : " Why could I not be seen by the people of that world wherein my husband dwells after the death of his Padma-body ?"

Saraswati answered : "Because thou wert not then as yet a Satya-Samkalpa (1), which condition is attained only by practice and the perfect realisation of Advaita, non-separateness, non-attachment to one single body, the not-feeling of an unbreakable identity with the body of Lila. Thou hast now become such a Satya-Samkalpa and if thou goest now to

(1) A state of consciousness in which things are seen as they are, in their true nature. Etymologically, 'one whose ideation becomes real, imagination true'.

that world of thy husband thou mayest be able to hold converse with him."

Lila: "What great wonder is this! In the space enclosed by these house-walls lived my husband the Brahmana. In this same space are situate the domains of Padma, and he lived and died in this. And in this same space, too, is he again a greater king with wider sovereignty.".

Saraswati: "Yes, O daughter! And yet at the same time are the three worlds distinct and separated by thousands of millions of Yojanas! Thus are there vast worlds all placed away within the hollows of each atom (1), multifarious as the motes in sunbeams. Which husband wilt thou go to now?"

(1) [Here we have an allusion to one of those occult truths that are what the French call *insaisisables* to the ordinary mind. The atomic sub-planes—I am obliged here to use the exact terminology of Theosophy—taken together make up one cosmic plane, that of Prakriti, and interpenetrate each other as do ethers, gases, liquids and solids here on our physical plane. A man able to rise to the state of consciousness (Satya-Samkalpa) in which a cosmic body is used would not need to "move" in order to be conscious of any point in the prakritic cosmic plane. Images of all the compounds into which they enter are thrown up in each atom, and he can study in the atom the existences of the plane to which the atoms belong. But if he goes out in a manasic Mayavi Rupa he may traverse the fields of space wherein are rolling worlds composed of the materials of the sub-planes of our planes, and so pass through thousands of millions of miles. Saraswati and Lila have been thus travelling, but Lila now discovers that she can by the Satya-Samkalpa vision, see the realms of Padma in the house of Vasishtha. An illusory sense of travelling may be felt in

Lila: "My memory comes back to me! Eight hundred births have I passed through, I see, since my descent from Brahma. I was the wife of a Vidyadhara (1) in the distant past. And step by step by growing grossness of desire I fell into vegetable and animal forms. I call to mind that I was once a creeper in a Muni's Ashrama (2). And by that holy influence I rose again. And once I was a king, and then I fell again because of sins. Aho! the marvels of these many births! I have slumbered sweetly as a bee on the soft petal of a lotus, and feasted to satiety on its pollen and its honey. As a bird I have struggled hard against and broken through the net of the horrible fowler, even as a weak man may break with difficulty through an evil addiction. From rock to rock have I leapt as a deer with beautiful eyes in the mind-stealing scenes of wooded hills, till I was shot down by the cruel

the karana sharira even without moving; for the mind seizes perceptions with incredible rapidity when freed from the heavy vehicles it uses in the lower worlds; when it opens up new avenues of perception objects flash along them, to which the mind successively responds and this gives a sense of motion. (Compare the illusory motion experienced by a person in a stationary train when a moving train passes). Consciousness may change without change of locality, and we are where we perceive, space being as illusory as time. A.B.]

(1) An aerial being.

(2) An ascetic's woodland abode.

arrow of the Kirata (1). I have also floated on the ocean billow as a huge turtle, and again as a giant fish. I have been a Pulindi (2) on the banks of the Charmanvati (3), singing and drinking the fresh juice of the cocoanut. I have known the deepest loves of youth on the golden and jewelled table-lands of Meru, and have also lain on costly couches shivering with sickness like a moon-beam on unsteady water.''

Conversing thus the two passed out of the house of the Brahmana, and Lila recognized the things of that past life of hers and pointed them out to the Goddess one by one. Then they went back to the house, and Lila, with her now enlightened eye, saw how the whole of the Padma-world was situate in a small part of that house-space, and said to the Devi : " Let us go back there." Then they returned to that other Brahmanda, going through the same long journey they had come, beholding again the wonders of space and feeling its endless expanse which, as Saraswati said, Gods higher than herself, Vishnu and Hara and others, could not measure, if they rushed through it all their life long.

Here Rama asked Vasishtha how such remoteness in space could be at the same time with such

(1) A hill tribe.
(2) Another hill tribe.
(3) A river in India.

nearness; and Vasishtha told him to consider how in dreams men with their bodies lying in one place still wandered over many lands and seas. And therewith he returned to the story of Lila.

Vasishtha continued:

Returning to the Padma-world, the two saw Lila's Chitta-body(1) sitting silent by the side of Padma's body resting on the fragrant flowers amidst the incense-scented air of the great palace-room. Seeing that body and her own Chitta-body, Lila thought she would now visit again that other world to which her husband had gone after leaving his Padma-form. And with the thought she passed, in her Sankalpa-deha, into that world, after piercing through the shells of that third Brahmanda as before. Saraswati went with her.

Arriving there within her husband's country, she saw a great battle impending between two vast armies arrayed in a forest that seemed extensive as space itself. Far as the eye could reach, the long lines of naked sword-blades, gleaming battle-axes, lances and arrow-points quivered and rattled with

(1) Chitta is distinct from Chit, and is to be used ordinarily for the mind with its three functions of knowing, desiring, and acting. It is practically the Jiva or Soul. It is never applied to Brahm, as is Chit. Here the body is the desire-body or astral.

the tense excitement of the warriors. A moment each proudly awaited the first stroke from the other, and then the two armies rolled into one with the roar of meeting oceans.

Lila saw it was her hero-husband righteously resisting the invasion of a hostile king. They only are the heroes—Shuras—who fight truly and honourably in a just cause or in obedience to their righteous king and master ; and such only go to heaven, not they who fight falsely, without good cause, however, brave (1).

And all day long the battle raged and roared ; and soon the ground was spread with mounds of dead, rising from thick unwholesome pools of blood and crushed and mangled flesh of men and beasts. The carcasses of elephants arose like islands from the surface of that sea of death ; and pieces of shattered cars drifted about like spars of storm-wrecked boats. And shrieks of agony rang everywhere, and cries for father, mother, brother, friend ; and frantic calls by leaders to their hosts to save the wounded and not trample down their own.

But with the sinking sun the slaughter slackened.

(1) It must be remembered that "righteous war" was the highest duty of the Kshattriya, the warrior, and death in such a war, as the gate of Svarga, might therefore well figure in a king's heaven.

The greater part lay dead or wounded. The rest were tired and worn. Emissaries went to and fro. Both sides agreed to cease hostilities for the night. White flags were floated out. Shortly the evening moon shone on a sickening scene of death and desolation, where the morning sun had lighted up a gorgeous show of bravery. Women wandered over the field of battle searching for their husbands, and when they found them dead, slew themselves with the weapons that had stricken their loved ones. Filthy carrion-beasts and creatures of the other spheres, Yakshas, Pishachas, Virupikas, Kumbhandas, Rakshasas and Putanas, Vetalas and Kushmandas (1), prowled about and fought amongst themselves over the corpses.

Leaving the scene of the battle, the two entered the palace where Lila's husband was seeking a moment's rest from the day's toil in sleep. They entered through the walls, which offered no obstruction to their subtle forms. There is obstruction only for the Adhi-bhautika (2) bodies filled with the fixed consciousness of length and breadth and grossness, filled with the thought, "I cannot enter here, I am resisted."

(1) Names for varieties of elementals and elementaries.

(2) Physical, composed of physical elements.

A holy influence spread through the sleeping-chamber of the king as the two beings entered it, and under its soft touch the king awoke with a new sense of gladness. He saw the two Apsara-forms [1] and offered them handfuls of flowers from the vase standing beside the bed, in welcome and in salutation. The king's chief minister, sleeping in that same chamber on that restless night, also awoke and greeted them.

The Goddess then addressed the king : "Who art thou, O king ?, and born of whom ?"

The minister answered for the king: "My master, the king Vidu-ratha, is the tenth descendant of king Kunda-ratha of Ikshvaku's line. And he and I have this day found the fruit of our past good deeds in this high and holy vision of you."

Saraswati addressed the king again : "Rajan ! call back to mind thy previous births," and laid her hand softly upon his head. And at the touch the darkness that enwrapped his heart gave way and luminous memory rose up within him. Reeling and swaying with the wonder of that memory, as on the surging surface of the ocean, the king exclaimed : "I see the overpowering Maya of Samsara ! What is this, O Devis ? It is not quite one day since I

(1) Celestial forms.

forsook in death my Padma-body, and yet I here have passed through seventy years of infancy and youth. I can remember my grandfather, and when I was but ten years old my father went away into the woods as a Pari-vrat (1), installing me as king, and many are the acts I have passed through. I see now that this present world of mine lies enclosed within the world of Padma, and that again within the world of Vasishtha; and also that the Kalpas of one world are fractions of the Kshanas of another (2). And all is the play of Consciousness."

"Yes, it is so," Saraswati said to the king, and added: "We would go now as we came. I came to thee at the request of Lila."

Here Rama asked a question of Vasishtha: From all this it would seem that the dream-world seen during sleep persists even after the sleeper has awakened! And Vasishtha answered him: Yes, it should be so, for wherein is the difference between the waking world and the dream world? The mutual relations of the seer and the seen, and also of the seer and the other men and women, are the same in both. And this is what Saraswati said to the king. And Viduratha begged of her that

(1) A wandering ascetic.

(2) The ages of one are the moments of another.

her compassion should not leave him profitless and that he too might go with them together with his young and childless wife and the minister.

Saraswati : " It shall be as thou wishest. Thou shalt go again to the Padma-world and animate again the corpse of Padma. But before this happens thou hast to die, warring against thy present enemy. The way is not the same for all."

And even as they were so talking, there entered at one side hurried messengers reporting that the enemy had broken into the capital, and at another came the youthful queen of Vidu-ratha, full of tears and terror, trembling in every beautiful limb and saying that the antah-paura [1] was also being attacked from behind.

Hearing these things the king arose in haste and said to the two Devis, " With your leave I will now go out to do battle with the enemy. This is my wife. May she remain near to your holy feet." And saying this, the king went out of the palace with flaming eyes like those of an angered lion.

Lila then noticed that the new-come queen was the very image of herself in outer appearance, and eagerly she turned to Saraswati and questioned. "How is this, O Devi ? How is there this double of my-

(1) The inner, or women's apartments.

self? How also are the ministers and many of the prominent citizens and warriors the same as in the Padma-world? How can these be in two places at the same time?"

Saraswati: "The consciousness, Jnyapti, realises its own objects. Chiti (1) takes on the form of its objects even as Chitta (2) takes on the form of its objects. Dreams are the apt example. Thy husband has attained here in this world the objects bearing which in mind he died in the Padma-world. Dreams are very real to the dreamer. They are all unreal to him when he wakes. So may the waking world be real and unreal. Such is the law of Pratibha—Imagination—which is of the nature of the all-pervading Atma. Whatever image arises as existent in the Vyoma (3) which constitutes the Atma of the king, that image also arises as true in the Ambara (space outside). This is how this second Lila appears by birth from reflection in the imagination (Pratibha). But soon thy husband Viduratha shall abandon his present body and go back to his old Padma-form."

The new Lila heard these words, and bending

(1) The higher consciousness.

(2) The desire mind.

(3) Literally atmosphere, but here the inner space which is fulness, sometimes called the Chid-akasha in the heart.

her head and folding her hands in soft entreaty, she spoke to Saraswati: " All my life have I worshipped the Goddess Saraswati with faith unswerving, and often she appears to me in dreams in the night. And as she is in my dreams such art thou in appearance now before me. I do believe thou art the same, and if thou wilt permit me I shall make now my long-deferred request."

Saraswati recalled to mind her long devotion, and said to her: " I am well pleased with thee; ask what thou wishest." And she asked: " Wherever my husband goes after abandoning his present body in battle, there may I too go in this same body of mine." And the Goddess said: " Yes."

The older Lila heard, and with doubt-shaken mind she asked the Goddess: " They that are Satya-Kamas (1) and Satya-Samkalpas (2) like thee, to them all things are easy. Why then, O Goddess! didst not thou take me in my old body to the village of the Brahmana, or bring him hither?"

Saraswati replied: "Lila of the bright complexion! I do not anything for anyone, in truth. It is the Jiva itself that procures all desires. I, Jnyapti, the Adhi-devata, the ruling Goddess of Consciousness,

(1) True-willed.
(2) True-imaginationed.

Samvit, simply give voice to it (1). The Chit Shakti (2) inheres in every Jiva as the power of that Jiva, and every Jiva secures its wishes by means of that power. Nothing gives anything to a Jiva except the persistent effort of its own consciousness. Its own Chit becomes the God that brings fruition of the effort. Thou ever cravest for Moksha in reality, and therefore have I taken thee through ways that will bring thee to that. Thou shalt learn more about this afterwards."

While the women were conversing thus, Viduratha fought with Sindhu in the night. And sounds of murder and of rapine rose upon the air. Houses caught fire. Women and children with their hair and clothes aflame ran helpless in their agony. Warriors died by thousands. But ever the clash and clang of arm and armour continued, and the force of Viduratha weakened. The two Lilas saw this, and asked Saraswati : " How is it, O Goddess !, that even with thy favour our husband prevails not over his foe ? "

And Saraswati answered : " Viduratha and his rival Sindhu both have made worship of me. And

(1) The Gods and Goddesses simply administer the law, bringing the man to the place where he meets the objects he desired. And so again below it is said that Saraswati can only give what is wished—not what is merely asked.

(2) Thought force.

the former ever carried wish for Moksha in his heart, and the latter wish for victory (1). And whatsoever the worshipper of me, Jnyapti, wishes of me, that only can I give to him."

And as they talked and the battle raged, the sun arose out of curiosity to see that sight. Bravely the king Viduratha fought as a Kshattriya and a king should fight, and many times he worsted his opponent Sindhu.

And after human weapons were exhausted, they fought with Astras (2) till both armies were destroyed. At the last, having consumed each other's war-cars with the Agney-astra (3), they fought again with swords till the keen straight edge of the sword was as the edge of a saw with the myriad dents of strokes of blade on blade. And in that combat Viduratha fell covered with wounds, and as his men brought up another car and tried to take him away, Sindhu made another stroke which nearly severed his head from his body. And in that state they brought the dying king into his palace, and there, beholding him, the younger Lila fell fainting upon the floor.

(1) A significant statement, throwing light on the "troubles of the righteous". If a man profoundly desires spiritual evolution, he must accept that which brings it, and worldly success hinders rather than helps.

(2) Celestial weapons.

(3) Fire-weapon—the "vril" of Bulwer Lytton.

The cry went forth that the king had been slain by the enemy, and all was terror and disorder in the city. Plunder and violence and lawlessness reigned for a while supreme. But shortly the victor-king was installed as Ruler of the country, and issued laws anew, and there was peace again.

Meanwhile Lila saw her husband lying all unconscious; only a breath remained in him. She spoke to Saraswati: " Mother! my husband is about to leave this body."

Saraswati: " Yea, so it is! But dost thou realise that all this fearful battle, all this city, all this world, is a mere dream existing in the space within thy palace in the Padma-world; that all that Padma-world again occupies but a small portion of the space within that little village-home ensconced amongst the Vindhya hills and tenanted of old by the Brahmana Vasishtha and his wife? All these three worlds, with thee and me and this, are dreams. All is illusion. Were there no dreamer there would be no dreams. Only the Atma is, and all this infinite display is its vibrations. There are whole worlds hidden away in single atoms (Chid-anu); and there are atoms in these worlds, and worlds again within these atoms, even as in the plantain-stem are folds in folds. Unto that one of all these endless worlds in which the body of Padma lies, the other Lila has gone on already. She reached it even when she swooned away at sight of the blood-covered body of Viduratha."

Lila: "Tell me, O Devi!, how she has gone on and how the denizens of that world behold her."

Saraswati: "Listen, and I shall say. All this world and its occurrences are experienced as a dream by Padma in that world. And that other Lila is his dream, as art thou too. Indeed we all are dreams unto each other. Only the being of the Great Consciousness (Maha-Chid-Jnyana-Samsthitih) gives being to us all. The reason of the consistency (Aika-matya, coincidence) of the thoughts of each and all is this: Each Jiva is the reflection of the Maha-Chit (the Great Consciousness), and the nature of that, which nature is the Great Destiny (the Maha-niyati), regulates and predestines all experiences of each and all, and thus all Jivas perceive each other mutually reflected (1).

(1) [This passage should be read with the later one (p. 107) on the awaking of Brahm: " And when it wakes again......sin and merit". The nature of things is due to the root-form assumed by the Divine Consciousness for a universe, and the similarity of the impressions of which Jivas are conscious is due to the relations established between them, and to their identity of inner nature. As hydrogen and oxygen brought from any distance will, under certain given condi-

"And so this other Lila has thy form because thy husband ever thought of thee, and she developed shape according to his thought. Then she worshipped me as thou hast done, and prayed not to be widowed any time. I granted her that prayer, and so she had to die before Viduratha and now she has passed on to the Padma-world, and there her form

tions, unite to form water, so will Jivas encased in similar vehicles receive from a given object similar impressions. These root-forms are imposed on the universe, and Jivas cannot get outside them, any more than they can escape from the Time and Space imposed on them, as limitations of consciousness. In fact, in every Jiva the one Self is thinking, feeling, acting, under these limits laid down for that universe at its inception; because of this, and because all are encased in vehicles shaped according to the root-forms, and are subject to the ideas of Time and Space, common ideas and common "sense" arise, causing an illusive feeling of reality. When the subject is studied on the manasic plane it is noticeable that the forms created by different Jivas of a common friend are by no means identical, although showing a broad similarity; each is an image, the reflection in manasic matter of that friend, due to the modification of consciousness caused by that friend in the seer's mind, and a ray from the Jiva animates each. In this there is nothing new, no increase of illusion. On the contrary, in the physical life these forms equally exist, and each man's concept of his friend is to him his friend himself; but on the physical plane this multiplicity is hidden by another veil of illusion, due to the sense-relation between the two physical forms of the friends; when this extra veil is removed, the multiplicity becomes patent. The reason why the multiplicity of forms does not arise here is the stubborness of physical matter. Long continued and strong thought may, however, produce a form, perceptible by the physical senses, the "double" of the original and in outer appearance indistinguishable from him. The phenomenon is rare, for it needs concentrated thought, and, where it has occurred, that concentration (at the present stage of evolution) has been brought about by passion.

is even as it was here. After quitting this body she went forth into space, and there she met a virgin whom I sent to guide her, and who led her through the stretches of this Brahmanda, through its elemental shells, into that other Brahmanda, where the Padma-world is situate. There she saw her husband, believing she still retains the body she was wearing here : and Padma, too, reviving, beholds her, and she and they and all the retinue about the palace regard each other as before the death-swoon of king Padma."

We may say that there is but one imagination, that of the Self, and each Jiva is as imagined by the Self (imagination-creation); then each Jiva, thus seen by the Self thinking as Jivas, appears in manifold reflections, as many as the Jivas with which he comes in contact, the variations being due to varieties in the mental media which reflect. Thus the moon is one, but may be reflected in the heaving sea, the quiet lake, the rushing torrent, the interstices of a weed-covered pond, a sheet of glass, a cup of ink, a piece of metal, a white wall, etc. Each of these reflectors, if capable of thought, could only be conscious of the moon as reflected in itself; the reports would be very different, yet the moon is one.

Looked at thus, the somewhat mysterious statement of Sarasvati (p. 98) "Whatever image arises as existent...from reflection in the imagination" becomes intelligible. There was one Jiva (called Lila) using the vehicles created by the imagination of the Jiva called Padma in the astral, Vidura-tha in the Manasic, world; so the vehicles Padma and Viduratha were created by the imagination of the Jiva called Lila in both worlds; the relation between the Jivas was enduring, the vehicles were merely the reflections in the outer space of the action in the consciousness of each due to that relation.

The worship of Sarasvati by the "two" Lilas and the prayer uttered by each are interesting as showing the identity of the Jiva manifested in both. A.B.]

Lila: " Why did she not go on in this same body? Such was thy boon to her."

Saraswati: " Unenlightened beings may not go to Siddha-worlds in their own bodies, even as shadows may not go into the sunshine. Such are the laws fixed at the first creation, and they may not be transgressed. While the man believes, 'I am composed of earth and cannot fly in space,' truly he cannot do so. It is enough that she believes that she has retained her own old body, this is all that can be done by boon or curse."

Saraswati continued : "They that know what it is fit to know and also give themselves up to the highest Dharma, they only gain the Ati-vahika worlds [1], not others. The Adhi-bhautika body, whose very nature is a false illusion—how may it endure in the true? The other Lila knows not that which should be known, but only clings unto what she thinks her highest duty, and therefore has she gone to her husband's imaginary city in the manner in which she has gone there."

Lila : "Aho! I understand this not. How came there to be a law ruling the birth and disappearance of things and how again an utter absence of such Law! How come Sva-bhavas, natures of things, to be

(1) The worlds beyond, the higher worlds.

so fixed? How is there Satta-existence in any objects? Why is fire hot and earth inert and the snow cold? What is the being of Time and Space? Whence these perceptions of existence and non-existence, of grossness and of subtleness? How came some things to grow upwards and high while some remain dwarfed and supine? Why and how are there any Laws of Nature?"

Saraswati: "During the reign of the great sleep of Maha-pralaya, Brahm alone remains as Endless Space and Peace supreme. And when it wakes again at the end thereof in the form of Chit (Consciousness), It thinks unto Itself, 'I am a speck of Light,' even as thou imaginest thyself of any form thou pleasest during dreams. That speck of light again assumes unto Itself Extension, 'I am large.' That mass, false in reality, becomes the Brahm-anda. Within that Brahm-anda, Brahm thinks again: 'I am Brahma,' and Brahma forthwith becomes the Ruler of a vast mental empire which is this world. In that first creation, Consciousness took many forms; and the root forms that Consciousness assumed in that Beginning—they persist unchangeably throughout the Kalpa. That is the Destiny which is the Nature and the Law of things, while that Primal Consciousness shall last. It makes what are our space and time and basic elements. It makes them what they are out of Asat [1].

That Destiny has also fixed the spans of human life, varying in various Yugas with variations in the grades of sin and merit."

Lila : "Tell me more of Death, O Mother !"

Saraswati : "Three are the kinds of men at time of death : (*a*) the ignorant ; (*b*) the man of practised Dharana (concentration) ; (*c*) the man of Yukti (developed reason, or Yoga). The latter two, after abandoning the body, go as they please. The first suffers. Tied to desires and longings unsatisfied, his condition is truly pitiable. With intelligence unpurified by Shastras [2], or by association with the good, he burns internally with terror and confusion, even as one fallen into the fire. After passing through the pains of dissolution he has memory of the past, and experiencing the swoon of death he beholds himself in another body, in another world, with sky, and moon, and day-light; and then is called Preta. Six degrees are there of the Pretas, with many further sub-divisions. The lowest, grossest, and most evil undergo a swoon, and imprisonment of consciousness as in the heart of a rock,

(1) Unreality, non-being.

(2) Scriptures, Sciences.

for a whole Vatsara (1). Others have pleasant times. And so each kind and grade of Preta has its own appropriate experience. And when their time is ripe, then on the shoulders of the wind and ether are they borne into the fruits and grains of cereals and plants, thence into the hearts of men, and finally into the wombs of mothers, whence they take their birth again as human beings. And all this process is repeated many times, till all shall pass into the final Peace, unswervingly, in the vast course planned out at the beginning of the Sarga (2) by the first Prajapati (3). In the meanwhile, most Jivas are self-centred so completely that they are oblivious of each other, and feel not each other's common Jiva-hood, even as men that dwell on the shores of the southern ocean know naught of the men that inhabit the shores of the northern, or as the toad that lives in the core of the mountain-stone knows not of the frog that croaks in the stream of the valley."

(1) Year.
(2) Manifestation.
(3) Lord of creatures.

CHAPTER VI

The Story of Lila (concluded)

Saraswati : "But see, the king Viduratha has almost passed away, and is even now entering again into the heart of the body of Padma lying on the flowers."

Lila : "Devi ! let us follow too by the same path by which he goes."

Saraswati : "He goes in the Chin-maya (1) form by the path laid out by his desire. Let it be as thou sayest ; we too shall go by the same way. To counteract each other's wishes would surely loosen all the bonds of love."

And as they spoke thus to each other, the eyes of the king Viduratha turned inwards ; the lips grew dry and white ; the whole frame took the colour of sere leaves, the breath came thin like the sounds of the wings of the tiniest bees, the limbs grew motionless like carven stone, and all at once the Jiva quitted that body as birds quit falling trees, and soared into the skies. With their luminous vision the two, Saraswati and Lila, saw the Jiva set itself upon the surface of a stream of air, and begin its long journey through the vast expanse of space. They follow-

(1) Astral body.

ed after it as two young bees a streak of fragrance stolen by the wind. Shortly the consciousness of the Jiva awoke with the oblations offered by Viduratha's relations, even as the sleeping scents of blooms awaken with the morning breezes ; and imagining a body to itself it saw the messengers of Yama (1) leading it to his abode. Yama saw the new arrival and said : "No evil acts are his, but only the good ones, and he has won the favour of Saraswati. He has to go again to the body of Padma. Let him go, therefore." And Yama's messengers permitted him to go ; and he, followed by the two others, swept on again through various regions till they came to the world, the lands, the capital and the palace of king Padma, and entered it as minute currents of air enter a budded lotus.

There they saw, sitting beside the body of Padma, and fanning it with a jewelled chamara (2), the Lila of the Viduratha-world, beautiful as there, wearing the same bright dress and ornaments, pale with intentness on her husband's face, voiceless, resting her cheek on her left hand, like the new-risen moon held on the edge of a tiny silver cloud on a starless night in the early spring.

(1) Death.
(2) Fan ; whisk, made of the tail-hairs of the chamari or yak.

They saw not the body which the enlightened Lila left behind when starting on her journey to the other world, and on being questioned Saraswati said to Lila : "These palace-maidens have been keeping watch over king Padma's body for a whole month now as they count their time, and thy old body fell lifeless after a fortnight. The ministers mourned over it, as for thy death, and gave it to the Sacred Fire, and did the last rites of the Vedas for it. Seeing thee again and the new Lila they shall only think that thou hast come back from the other world by a great miracle and brought a fair companion with thee too. Their thought shall reach no further."

With this the two made themselves visible to the new Lila. Startled from her reverie by that sudden light that filled the room, washing its walls with liquid gold and making it look as if hewn out of the moon, she saw the glorious forms and prostrated herself before them, and then explained that she had come on in advance of them after her temporary swoon, and had seen her husband sleeping after the fatigue of the battle and so had not awakened him.

Saraswati then permitted the Jiva of Viduratha, whom she had detained for a while, to enter into the heart of Padma through the nostrils ; and it entered there, carrying within it its hundred Vasanas, desires, even as the ocean carries in its deep heart its treasured gems. And therewith, like a withering lotus at the touch of the first rain-drops, the body of Padma revived, in the limbs flowed the sap of life again, and they shone forth with recovered softness and brilliance like new leaves under the breath of spring. He unclosed his eyes, beautiful and pure, with starry pupils ; rose, towering like the Vindhya mountain ; and, sitting up in bed, called "Who is there ?" in tones sonorous as the distant thunder. The two Lilas advanced and bent before him. Seeing these two beautiful images of each other, the king was much astonished and enquired what had happened. The elder Lila then explained : " I am thy elder queen, O husband !, bound unto thee inseparably as word to meaning ; and I have earned for thee thy second queen, this younger Lila. (1) And she that sits on the great throne of gold beside thy couch is the Goddess Saraswati, by whose favour we all meet again". The king arose and bowed at the feet of the Goddess, and prayed : "O Goddess !, give us wisdom and enlightenment." And Saraswati

(1) Lila means Play, Pastime. The world-process is the Self's Play, Pastime, Drama. To *know* it as Play, is Wisdom, Vidya, the enlightened Lila ; to *feel* it as real, is error, A-vidya, the younger Lila. The former carries the latter. Win God, and all things else add themselves.

blessed them all and departed, saying: "Be ye happy." And thereafter all was gladness and rejoicing throughout the kingdom, and people wondered and conversed amongst themselves how the great love of the queen had brought back the king and her own Jiva twofold from the other worlds. And the king and the two Lilas reigned wisely and well, for eight myriads of years, and then all passed into the peace of Videha-mukti. (1)

CHAPTER VII

Consciousness

Vasishtha said: Thou must have gathered from the tale of Lila, which I told to thee, O Prince !, that the feeling of solidity which makes the world around seem independent in its realness is also but mere Consciousness, as much as the feeling of tenuity or liquidity. All this multifarious universe is nothing else than the play of a Single Point of Consciousness, which encloses and contains within itself all Self and all Not-Self and all their mutual interplay, past, present, and to come. What the Consciousness imagines strenuously that it feels as real. If it will imagine to itself a solid body

(1) Liberation.

standing before the impassable barrier of a wall of rock, to that body the rock is truly an impassable barrier. If it will, by equal stress, eliminate solidity from both, they will no longer be a bar and a resistance to each other. If it will rush through the whole experiences of a Kalpa in a single moment, that single moment is verily a Kalpa. If it will spread leisurely the experience of a single moment over the time covered by a whole Kalpa, then that Kalpa is, to that Consciousness, no more than a single moment. Lavana passed through a hundred years of life in a single night. What is but a Muhurta (1) to the Lord of creatures, Brahma, that is the whole lifetime of a Manu; what is the whole lifetime of a Brahma is but as a day to Vishnu of the Discus; and what, again, is the whole life-period of a Vishnu is but a day of Maheshvara of the Bull (2). And he who is firm-fixed in Nirvikalpa-Samadhi (3) knows neither night nor day; time and lapse of time are naught to him. See, in this world, how Consciousness doth ever make reality. Practice

(1) A period of time equal to forty-eight minutes.

(2) Ordinarily, the Puranas indicate that the Brahma, Vishnu and Shiva of each world-system are co-evals and compeers. But the Vishnu of a larger system may have many Brahmas of smaller systems within His jurisdiction; and so the Shiva of a still larger system may rule over many smaller Vishnus; and so on indefinitely. Some of the visible stars are millions of times larger than our sun.

(3) Meditation without a definite object.

makes sweet bitter, bitter sweet. Persistence changes foe to friend and friend to foe. Strange things, new sciences, the ways of Japa and of meditation seem so hard at first; practice, persistent Consciousness, makes them all easy.

And, yet, remember that the Great Consciousness imagines all things equally. As within limited times and spaces, the weaker individual consciousnesses follow unresistingly the lead of the more powerful, even as thin streaks and lines of air are driven along by the torrent-mass of the cyclone, so the Great Consciousness of the One Self directs the entire movement of the world. That All-guiding Consciousness is one, and everywhere unbroken, throughout the endless universe, wherein the worlds arise and disappear without beginning and without an end, like seed and plant in never-closed rotation.

We have looked outwards for so long, we have almost forgotten that there is an inner; and far more difficult is it now for us to realise that both the outer and the inner are maintained, supported, nay, in very truth, created, by our Consciousness. Ponder long and deeply on the unbroken nature of Consciousness. Even in a single human being, although we may for certain purposes distinguish layers and different constituents, yet, in the deepest sense, the whole nature of man is one. Even as there is no difference between Chid-Atma (Universal Self and Consciousness) and the individual Jiv-atma, so is there none between a Jiva and its Chitta (mind). And even as there is no separateness and difference between the Jiva and its Chitta, so is there none between the Chitta and the Deha (body). And lastly, as there is no separateness and difference between the mind and the body, so is there none between the body and its various actions. All is Consciousness.

Listen to another tale.

CHAPTER VIII

The Story of Karkati; her hunger and austerities

Karkati, the Rakshasi, dwells on the northern slopes of the Himalaya mountains. Black and fearsome is she, as dire statues carved from the sheer side of a mountain of soot petrified. Gaunt is her frame, like the drought-dry forests of the Vindhya hills. Mighty is she, and her eyes are as flaming fire, for never is her hunger satisfied. Black is her garment, too, as if woven out of the densified nights of the rainy season. Fogs and mists enwrap her; and clouds rest on her head. Bones and skulls bedeck her fearsomeness.

The meat that she obtains extinguishes not the fire of her hunger, even as the ever-pouring stream of salt waters quenches not the fire of the seavolcano. And, therefore, she once thought within herself: "If I could only swallow all the teeming people of the land of Jambu-dvipa (1) in a process as unceasing as my breath, then, perchance, my hunger would be stayed. And yet it is not easy to prevail against a people guarded well by mantras (2), medicines, clean ways, and charities and worship of the gods. But Tapas (3) brings about things most improbable; therefore, let me make great Tapas."

Ascending a tall peak untrodden by other creatures, she stood on a single foot, immovable, till she became as a part of the rocks around. A thousand years elapsed, and Brahma, Cosmic Mind Embodied, came, constrained by that long self-denial, to bestow on her the boon she craved. "O daughter Karkati!, thou art the glory of the Rakshasa race," He said; "name the boon thou cravest." She pondered long and then replied: "O Father of Creation!, may I at will become a living needle with two

(1) Asia.
(2) Magic chants.
(3) Austerity, penance.

forms, one gross and one not such; and may I have the power at will to enter into the hearts of creatures and suck away their lives." "Be it so," He said, and added: "Thou shalt be a Soochika (1) with an upasarga (2); men shall call thee Vi-shoochika (3). In subtle form shalt thou des troy all beings that live on unclean foods, go evil ways, are foolish and ill-balanced. Thou shalt prevail against them that dwell in foul places and act in foul ways. Thou shalt enter into them, even into their heart, and seizing on the lotuses (4) and the spleen and other organs, thou shalt slay and devour them. But if thou shouldst, by some mischance, attack the good and virtuous, then shall this mantra help them to get rid of thee, and thou shalt fly back from them to these mountains (5)." And Brahma uttered the strong mantra there, and Siddhas floating by recorded it, and Brahma, too, went back to His Abode.

(1) A needle.

(2) 'Upasarga" means a "prefix" in grammar; it also means a "discharge," "an excrescence," "a protrusion".

(3) An infectious disease, generally the cholera; also a form of the plague; the naming after the "needle" seems to have reference to the shape of the disease-microbe. The mention of fogs and mist and clouds in the description of Karkati, similarly seem to refer to the seasons and physical conditions in which epidemics are most violent.

(4) Ganglia, glands, plexuses.

(5) Some varieties of the plague are said to be endemic in the hills.

CHAPTER IX

The Transformations of Karkati and further Tapas

Forthwith the mountain-large frame of Karkati began to shrink. In a moment it looked like only a great black cloud ; then, a tree ; shortly, like a human being ; next instant it was but a span high ; again, but as a grain of mustard ; then as a dot of the sapphire-ray of the sun ; and finally, invisible like space itself. Beautiful and subtle as the Brahm-nerve (Sushumna) out on its way through the Brahm-randhra ([1]) to the sun, she floated in mid-space, like the drying tress-points of a fresh-bathed maiden.

Behold the wonders of intentness in excess on any single thing ! So full was Karkati's consciousness of hunger and its satisfaction, she minded not her own great body falling off and leaving her so small and insignificant. And full of that same consciousness she roamed, and roamed in her double form, appearing now as Ati-vishoochika and now Antar-vishoochika ([2]), ever insatiate of the lives that she

(1) A passage through the brain and the top of the skull known to the science of Yoga.

(2) Literally "excessive Vishoochika" and "internal Vishoochika", a reference probably to various forms of the disease. The cholera and the plague have for long been the two chief scourges of the East.

destroyed. Doing her fell work she wandered over the face of the earth, driven away, now and again, when she attacked the righteous, by acts of charity and mantras, medicines and tapas. For many years she wandered thus, hiding in the dust and hidden from the light, skulking in human limbs and organs tainted with unclean living, flourishing in heaps of filth, in dried-up ditches, and in rotten straw.

At last she grew tired of her troubled life, uncertain hiding-places, and the constant struggle ; and the thought arose within her mind and gathered strength as she dwelt on it : "Did I do well to change my immense form for this small one ? The tiniest drop of food now overfills me, and I no longer know the taste of those large mouthfuls of delicious meats of old. I hide about in mud and mire and unclean places. Shall I remain much longer in this state ? O my great legs ! with which I stepped with ease from peak to peak of these vast mountain ranges ! O beautiful black nails ! that tore down rocks in play ! O stomach ! roomy like the mountain-gorge ! O large and beauteous face ! the broadening smile of which stampeded even my fellow Rakshasas with terror ! O arms ! the weight of which broke down the mountain-pines ! O eyes ! that set the darkness of the night on fire ! Why did I ever part with you ? Alas ! Why did I give you all away for this contemptible needleness that even the hoof of a fly can fling away ? Alas ! when shall I get you back again ?"

Silently she suffered, till in the intensity of her remorse it came to her that as she lost her giant body, so, by those same means, she might recover it again. Therewith she went back to the self-same mountain peak on which she first performed her long austerities, and stood again on a single tiny foot fixing it deep into a single grain of granite to avoid being blown away by the winds. Thus she stayed for full seven thousand years, flooded by the torrents of the rains, swayed by mighty tempests, roasted by forest-fires, pelted by hail, dazed by the lightning, interrupted in her meditations by the thunder of the clouds, yet never shaken from her purpose and her place. With the lapse of that long time and with the pressure of her manifold experience, a wonder and a restlessness of thought arose within her, and she reflected deeply on the nature of the world and of the Self. She pondered for a thousand years on the great mystery, until she saw that very nature of the Self, containing all the world within itself. That final knowledge rose all luminous within her, under the unremitting stress of the

Self-reflection, than which there is no higher Teacher of deeper truth to the Jiva; and the long Tapas came unto its ripening.

The mountain glowed with its glory, and Indra, the King of the gods, enquired of Narada, their Sage, whose strong penance was so potently enveloping the worlds in overpowering blaze, converting the cool caves of the Abode of Snow into hiding-places of heat untenable by the gods. Narada explained; and Indra went at once to seek for remedy from Brahma, praying him to grant the wished-for boons of Karkati. Brahma gave assent, and came to Karkati, and said: "Ask, daughter, for the thing that thou desirest." Reduced to the merest of the subtlest streak of the Jiva-consciousness, devoid of organs, she could make no answer, and only thought within herself: "What do I want that feel the fulness of the Self? I want no boons. I know all there is to be known; my doubts are fled; I stand in perfect peace; likes and dislikes have disappeared; all is as one to me." Rejoicing at her mood, the Lord of Creatures said: "'Tis well that all is one to thee, my daughter! Thou desirest neither to accept nor to reject. Then let the laws of limited nature take their course. The Tapas-Karma thou hast done requires a consequence. So live some further time upon the earth in thine old great frame, developing it anew from this thy present tininess, as forest-giants grow from subtle seeds. But having seen the Truth, thou couldst not take to evil ways again, and cause the innocent to suffer. So I ordain that for thy sustenance thou shalt feed only on the sinful and impure. When thou hast thus exhausted all thy karma and lived, a Jivan-mukta (1) through thy life, then shalt thou go to the Abode of Bliss."

With this He disappeared ; and in a moment Karkati passed back from the size of a sunbeam-mote, to seed, span, cubit, human stature, towering tree, and finally to that of a giant mountain-peak again.

CHAPTER X

The Question of the Rakshasi

A touch of pleasure passed into her illumined mind at the regaining of her former frame ; but in a moment she threw off the insidiously-reviving pride of Rakshasa-hood, and passed into Samadhi. Six months passed away ; and then the body awoke and asserted its claims for nourishment, as it always will while life has not departed. Then she wondered:

(1) Free while still living in the body.

"I cannot eat unrighteous food again. It matters not to me whether this body live or die. Had I not rather let it die away ?" But Nabhasvan the Wind, came to her help, seeing her fixed so firmly in resolves of right, and spoke unseen : "Wander forth, O Karkati !, bestowing knowledge on the ignorant. There is no truer charity, no more precious gift, than the gift of Self and of Self-knowledge. He who gains it gains the universe. He gains assurance of his deathlessness ; and to the strength of that great confidence, all labours, losses, pains are light and easy. Therefore walk the world, O Rakshasi !, endeavouring to spread Self-knowledge. And those that turn away persistently from it shall be fit food for thee. Receiving not the Self but throwing it away, themselves they do destroy themselves, and so no sin shall come to thee in eating them."

She thanked the Wind, rose straight like a colossal water-spout from the disturbed surface of the ocean, descended slowly from the peak into the valleys, and entered the habitation of a tribe of Kiratas (1) dwelling at the foot of the mountains.

Night reigned there at the time. Clouds hid the moon and stars. The darkness hung so dense it could be almost pushed about by the hands. In that

(1) A hill-tribe.

fearful night, Vikrama, the king of the tribe, was out with his prime minister to see that none disturbed the sleep of his people. Karkati beheld the two and thought: "Here is the food I look for. Let me see, though, that they have no virtue which prevents my swallowing them." To test them she let forth a hideous roar followed by harsh words, as a crack of lightning followed by a shower of hail: "What wandering worms are ye? Are ye wise? For I devour you else!"

The king replied: "Seek not to frighten us with empty sound, but show thyself, whoever thou art; then we shall judge how to behave to thee."

Thereat the Rakshasi displayed her fearful form, that used to strike with terror even her companion-Rakshasas. But the pure-minded know no fear; and the minister addressed her calmly:

"I see thou wantest food! Why then such great excitement for such little cause? If thou wouldst state thy wish more peacefully, it were more easy to fulfil it. The king accustoms not to turn away the really needy."

Then the Rakshasi reflected: "Their faces, eyes and speech, show me that these two are no common men, but knowers of the truth; so let me question further." And she asked aloud: "Tell me first who you are, and what you are doing here at this time of the night."

The minister explained and said: "We are abroad for the restraint of such as you from doing harm to our people."

The Rakshasi: "O king and minister !, prove to me that you deserve your offices, or I shall swallow both of you unfailingly. The Science of the Self is the highest of all sciences, and king and minister that know it not are not deserving of their offices. Tell me then what is that single atom in which millions of Brahmandas hide as bubbles in the ocean ? Describe to me that which is spaceless space; thing without substance; I and thou at once; that which stands still while ever moving; intensely living though dead as the rock; a blazing fire that will not burn; light and the source of light though all unseen; the light by which all blind things, climbing creepers, sprouting seeds and upward-pushing plants, all see their way unerringly; which yet is the very depth and density of darkness, too; a flashing moment longer than the endless Kalpas; an endless Kalpa, though but a flashing moment; which, evident to the senses, is yet nought; and which, again, is verily everything, though unperceived of any sense;

which, present everywhere, may not be grasped by hands, searching through myriad births; which thrusts itself into those very hands insistently, when they have ceased from search; a thing with million hands and feet and eyes, and yet devoid of limbs; a thing devoid of hands which yet paints living forms on the blank sheet of emptiness; which acts and moves and lives without a cause or motive; which makes a multifarious spectacle of its sole Self; which carries all the past, the present, and the future of all worlds, concentred in a single point within itself? What is that which has spread out this giant panorama of the universe? What is that, essenced with which, thou playest, slayest, guardest? What is that, by sight of which thou art annihilated into deathless being? What is that, which is both being and non-being? Resolve this little doubt of mine, O king and minister! They only are the wise who can supply solution of the doubts of those who question them. They are the foolish who have made themselves the slaves of sense. Are ye the latter, or are ye the former? If the latter, then, without a doubt, I swallow you, and all your people, too, thereafter. Unhappy, undeserving, unpossessed of acts of past good karma, vacant of acts of merit are the people that are governed by a foolish, vicious king."

CHAPTER XI

The Answer

As the great sounds of the Rakshasi's speech subsided like the roll of thunder dying away in the distance, the minister took up the answer, for when the lower in rank can carry out a work successfully, it is not right to trouble the higher. "Listen, O beauteous maid of nimbus-size and hue !, as I expound the answer to the question in a word. As thou thyself well knowest, in thy paradoxes thou hast spoken of the Supreme Self, the Param-atma, that shoreless Ocean of all Consciousness, in which intelligences form and disappear in countless numbers, like to vortices and whirlpools in the sea. Itself beholds Itself ; none else is there to do so. It is the resting-place of all things contradictory, all pairs of opposites, antagonists ever-lastingly. It moves and lapses not in space and time and motion ; for all space and time and motion are themselves within its changeless being. It has no motive to new act ; all acts and motives are within Its movelessness. The mother with the babe hid cosily between her breasts needs not to seek for it elsewhere. And if thou close and seal a bowl and carry it a hundred miles, how can thou say whether the space enclosed within the bowl has travelled also all the hundred miles or not ?

The Consciousness of a Kalpa is a Kalpa; the Consciousness of a moment is a moment. Consciousness of far and near is far and near. Apart from Consciousness naught is; within it are both aught and naught; both being and non-being".

The minister ceased; whereon the Rakshasi: "So pleasing is this talk to me, I would it were continued. Will then the king please to prolong it further?"

The king smiled and replied: "Let it be so! Most wondrous is that all-pervading Consciousness whose sole form and belief is the belief of the non-being of this universe (1); whose one Eternal Thought and vow is ab-negation of these Falsehoods of Imagination. It is the final goal of all the speech of the Vedanta; yet it is beyond all speech. Ever it dwells in the exact between of every pair of opposite extremes, including in itself, as mean, both these extremes. This Consciousness alone is the final and the efficient cause as well as the material cause of all this drama of the world. Its Unity remains unbroken though identical with all the endless Multiplicity of Kosmos. Such is the eternal Brahm that thou hast described, O virtuous maid! It is the Atom; it is also the Vast All. It is the Self; it is the Not-Self too, but everlastingly denied. Its

(1) "I-This-Not"; see *The Science of Peace* for detailed exposition of the idea.

Consciousness in the one Cause of causes. It is the very Self of every being, without the finding of which there is no peace throughout a hundred or a thousand lives of strenuous effort; and yet, with the finding of which naught new is gained, except final Deliverance from all doubt".

CHAPTER XII

The end of Karkati's story

All thought of harming them the Rakshasi abandoned finally on hearing the wise words of the king, even as the summer-heated earth throws off its fever with the fall of the first cooling drops of rain. A great joy arose within her mind even as the moon within the darkness of a tropic night. Her mood was beautified and softened as black rain-clouds by the rhythmic flights of lines of snow-white herons. She said to them :

"I am happy to have found you in this forest. Your minds are pure and lighted with the sun of quenchless wisdom. I would be friends with you. Can I perform some service?"

The king replied: "My people suffer from diseases of the heart, and various pains. Physicians are of no avail. They only say it is Vi-shoochika.

This is one reason why I sally forth of nights in hopes to meet with such as you, that either cause the ravage or may help to cure it. If you are the former then would I war with you with all my might; but if the latter, then I entreat your help in all humility".

The Rakshasi explained how she herself was the fell Vi-shoochika, unfolding all her story. The king prayed to her on the ground of new-made friendship that she desist from causing suffering to men. And she consented saying: "It is right; and I will go back to the mountain and cast off this ever-hungry frame of mine rather than slaughter human beings". But the king was much perplexed and said: "While it is right that you should not molest the innocent, it is not right that the immediate consequence of your acquaintance with me should be death to you. One way appears to me in which both ends may be secured. The criminals among my subjects, judged worthy of death, shall be reserved for you, and you shall come to me from time to time, slaying the wicked, nourishing yourself, helping the good and innocent, as those wise with the final wisdom ever should".

They parted in much mutual satisfaction with this compact; and in after times Karkati visited the king at the fixed times for food, spending the intervals in Yoga and Samadhi, by the power of which she guarded the king's people from superphysical ills. And when the king Vikrama passed away she was as friendly to his descendants for many generations. When she herself wore out her Rakshasa body and so visited them no more, then the people made a temple to her, giving her the name of Kandara, and also Amangala, under which names she is still worshipped in the mountains, as the guardian-goddess of the mountain tribes.

Vasishtha added: " This tale may help thee, Rama, in the understanding of how the body and the surroundings of the body change with the changes of the Manas-mind, how the giant hunger for the experiences of a grosser and more definite kind lead on the jiva from the subtler to the denser planes of nature; and how, again, when the jiva tires of those denser gains and pains, a converse hunger takes it back to those same planes of vast and subtle matter".

"Some little part I do begin to see," said Rama, " of how essential Consciousness is, to the universe. But tell me, Master!, how this changeful mind arises".

" I asked that question once, myself, of Brahma,' said Vasishtha, "and the story that he told to me in answer, I will relate to thee some other time".

Printed by K. P. Dar at the Allahabad Law Journal Press, and Published by The Indian Bookshop, Theosophical Society, Benares